WHAT I LEARNED FROM
3 DOGS IN 3 DAYS

NUGGETS OF WISDOM FOR A HAPPIER LIFE

A.P. Morris

Synchronistic Books
East Valley of Phoenix, Arizona
www.synchronisticbooks.com

What I Learned from 3 Dogs in 3 Days
Nuggets of Wisdom for a Happier Life

Copyright © 2019 by A.P. Morris
All Rights Reserved.

This book may not be reproduced, transmitted, or stored in whole or in part by any means, including graphic, electronic, or mechanical without the express written consent of the publisher except in the case of brief quotations embodied in articles or reviews where proper credit is given.

The author has represented full ownership and/or legal right to publish all the materials in this book.

Photo Editor: Cassandra Butler
Cover & Layout Design: Jera Publishing

Library of Congress Control Number: 2019918502

Synchronistic Books 2019
ISBN: 978-0-9854893-2-8

Printed In The United States of America

Dedication

To Butters, Lucy, Coco, and all of the dogs I've been lucky enough to know–thank you for allowing me to experience your unconditional love and continually learn through your beautiful hearts and souls.

Contents

Prologue	....	1
1	A Three Dog Night	5
2	It's a Dog's Life	13
3	Hot Diggity Dog	25
4	Doggone it!	37
5	Dog-Doo	47
6	Dog Eat Dog	57
7	Dog Days	67
8	Underdog	75
9	Dog and Pony Show	81
10	Be like a dog with two tails	91
11	Downward Dog	101
12	For the Love of Dogs	111
Epilogue	....	121
Acknowledgements	....	127
About the Author	....	129
Notes	....	131

Prologue

To my surprise, watching three dogs for three days during the last Thanksgiving holiday taught me substantially more than I bargained for. With each dog demonstrating distinct personalities and habits acquired from three different owners, I found myself paying close attention to their interactions with one another.

Mind you, this was an unplanned event. Typically, I get overwhelmed rather easily and wouldn't have scheduled having three dogs, two of which weren't mine, while cooking for three days straight. I was not hosting a Thanksgiving dinner but instead, pre-cooking a huge Italian meal for two separate occasions—a dear friend's birthday and my daughter's college graduation. This Italian cooking extravaganza only happens about once a year in my house, so I make enough to feed a small army with leftovers to freeze. It's quite a process that literally takes me three days to complete.

For what felt like 72 straight hours, I was either cooking or taking care of the dogs and napping in between. This experience was akin to an immersion study of canine behaviors. Not because I wanted to prove or disprove theories, because I'm not quite that smart. But, almost immediately it became a study of sorts when a seasoned male voice, pointing out the particulars, suddenly began speaking into my right ear.

I'm clueless as to the identity of the narrator, who reminded me of an audio book author with a very important caveat—I couldn't stop him, push pause, or play him back when it was more convenient. Whenever he felt compelled, he began speaking at a brisk pace and either I had to begin taking it down or as they say, I was shit-out-of-luck. I'm sure anyone who saw me walking three dogs while typing furiously with my thumbs on a cellphone thought I was nuts. Yes, really, a good portion of this book was typed in the notes app on my phone.

Although it was exhausting, my extreme gratitude prevailed. If you've ever written, let alone had a helpful voice assist you, you know it's a gift that you take when it comes. The bulk of the insight found within the following

Prologue

pages was given to me during those three days, although it piqued my interest so much that even after my invisible friend's voice fell silent, the observational perspective he awakened in me remained. There are still moments while walking alone with my dog, Butters, when I notice behaviors that could be related to human interactions, albeit minus the lovely narration.

CHAPTER 1
A Three Dog Night

"The saying 'a three dog night' hearkens back to precentral heating days when dogs were used by their owners to provide additional warmth on cold nights."[1] Personally, I need my space and although my dog sleeps in my bed, for the most part unless we are cuddling, he isn't close enough to provide warmth. For some, this could be considered an extra bonus but it is definitely *not* what comes to mind for many of us when we think of all the reasons we love our canine companions today.

There are a plethora to list, but the basis is that our dogs love us no matter what we look, feel, or act like on any given day. Even when we are grumpy, ignore them, or raise our voices, they don't hold a grudge. Without fail, they are always happy to see us when we come home, regardless of how long we were gone. Not to mention, they make us laugh and help us connect to the best parts of ourselves. I could go on forever but you get the gist—dogs are the epitome of pure, unadulterated love.

I don't know about you, but I LOVE my dog Butters, just as much as my beloved fur babies that came before him, especially Angel and Sara. Yes, I have a grown daughter so I'm intimately familiar with the depths of love a parent has for a child, it is incomparable. However, having experienced both, I have to admit there is something indescribably special about the relationship between a human and their dog.

Maybe it's because unlike children, dogs never outgrow snuggling. Or, that no matter what type of day they had or how old they get, dogs are always overjoyed to see us. If a greater power offered us a better example of what unconditional love looks like, I've never seen it. Don't you think it is a bit too coincidental that *dog* spelled backwards is *god*? I do. Personally, I think our canine friends are the embodiment of that love, gifted to us and wrapped in a varying assortment of fur.

Without hesitation, I submit that being a dog owner has made me a better person. Offering my imperfect love to a completely dependent and unconditionally loving soul has caused me to see the world in a different light. This epiphany may have always swirled in the background of my awareness, but thanks to my invisible friend, who shared three days of even deeper insights through these three beautiful dogs' behaviors, I love them even more. Mostly, because there couldn't be a more adorable vessel to deliver this awareness. It surely wasn't because they were perfectly behaved the entire time, they were not.

But, that is the first profound nugget I learned—*nothing in life is ever perfect, and the sooner we drop the misconception that it is supposed to be, the happier our lives become.*

So, how did a mother of a single child, and more recently a single dog, end up with three dogs for three days? I'm sure many of you have multiple dogs and are thinking what's the big deal? Numerous friends and acquaintances of mine have multiple dogs or children so I am aware of how much

Nugget #1

Nothing in life is ever perfect, and the sooner we drop the misconception that it is supposed to be, the happier our lives become.

more difficult it can be than raising one. I still remember years ago, while grocery shopping with my Nana, I asked how she had managed to take all seven of her children to the store with her to buy food. She demonstrated how the two smallest sat up front in the cart, three of the others stood on the sides and back, while the oldest two walked and helped retrieve the groceries. I couldn't imagine because parenting one child was hard enough for me.

Although you probably haven't heard many regret having their beloved bundles of joy, mothering is certainly exhausting and many days thankless. If the extra work, cost, and time isn't enough, let's not get started on the teen and young adult years. Anyway, you get the point—it's a lot of work regardless of the size of your family, but I have to say that I was always intimidated by taking care of more than one child, especially with my daughter's chronic health problems. Although I've wanted to add another dog to our family that is probably why we still only have one at a time as well. I'm worried it will be too much for me.

So, as you can see, it wasn't my original plan to have three dogs for three days. It just kind of happened when I ended up having my daughter's dog, Coco, for longer than I anticipated because her canine brother fell ill. She had been staying with us for over a week when it was time for Lucy to join us so her mother could work out of state for three days. My dear friend, Geani (aka Lucy's mom) and I excitedly kicked things off by celebrating Butters' third birthday on Wednesday afternoon. We took them to the park and watched them all run off-leash with wild abandon, playing non-stop for a couple of hours. Of course afterward, there was singing, a doggie birthday cake, presents, and goodie bags for each containing treats and a toy. Yes, Geani and I gladly go overboard, probably more for us than them, except the cake—they definitely loved it!

Maybe I was just as excited to have time off work, but it felt like the perfect beginning to a three-day slumber party where I planned to continue the fun festivities. Obviously, there really isn't much I wouldn't do for my baby boy. Don't scoff and pretend…I know I'm not alone in the crazy-things-we-do-for-our-babies department to express our adoration and make them happy. Whether they are our canine or human babies, we feel compelled to show them how much we love them. Especially during holidays, when we smile through the weariness while attending to endless cooking and entertaining, when you feel as if you are going to fall on your face at any moment.

I'm pretty sure my anxiety at times borders on OCD on top of dealing with chronic health conditions that limit my access to energy and stamina, so imagine my surprise when in addition to extensive cooking and dog sitting fun, I had this idea, or more accurately this mystery man's voice sprung up out of nowhere. Before he began speaking, I had no idea that I was about to observe and rapidly notate the good, bad, pretty, and ugly of interpersonal relationship behaviors, demonstrated by these three dogs over the next three days.

What an incredible gift! It did not escape me that this began on Thanksgiving, a time to be grateful for all of the blessings we have—seen and unseen. There was no other option for me but to embrace the voice, rapidly manifesting ideas, and note what he was saying as it related to the dogs' behaviors. I have to say for most of the three days, I was thoroughly exhausted and basically running on fumes, but I chose to focus on cooking delicious homemade Italian food from my maternal roots and enjoying the craziness of these dogs.

The thought also occurred to me afterward that the fatigue probably allowed me to let down my defenses so I wouldn't rationalize away my new friend's insight. I mean, I love learning about alternative spirituality, the possibilities of synchronicity, and had experienced intuition, but I'd never had a distinct voice speak in my ear before. To say it was a bit strange is an understatement, but who was I to look a gift horse in the mouth. Besides, being so busy didn't allow much time to debate my sanity.

While watching the dogs interact, they seemed unaware that they were acting out scenarios that appear in all of our lives as Morgan Freeman narrated. Well, it was a nice voice but I have to admit, in my opinion, no one's voice ever quite lives up to Mr. Freeman's—which is as unique and beguiling as they come.

Nevertheless, my faceless friend spoke in unison with the tiny, furry actors and it was nothing less than riveting to behold. This three day event resembled listening to an audio book that coincided succinctly with a live canine stage play. If you'd been able to watch this unfold, the funniest part was me trying like hell to type as fast as possible into my notepad app on my phone.

With great humbleness, I must clearly state that I can't take credit for most of the beautiful demonstrations to come. All that I did was open my home and heart to three beautiful fur balls, didn't check myself into a padded cell when a voice began speaking into my right ear, and agreed to pay attention and take stellar notes. Well, and all of the organizing, writing, editing, and publishing aspects but really, I feel more like the humble servant to this, rather than the creator.

Which leads to nugget number two—*opening your heart to others, by simply showing up ready to learn from them, is truly a secret recipe to rapid growth.*

Nugget #2

Opening your heart to others, by simply showing up ready to learn from them, is truly a secret recipe to rapid growth.

CHAPTER 2
It's a Dog's Life

In the past, 'it's a dog's life' is a saying that was used to express when something was considered hard and unpleasant. The dictionary explains, "the expression was first recorded in the 16th-century describing the miserable subservient existence of dogs during that era."[2] I don't know about your dogs or ones that you know, but these days, many dogs have quite the opposite experience.

I've always said that it would be darn near perfect if we do have to return to Earth again, to come back as a dog in a loving home. What could be better than spending your day napping in the sun, having your meals and treats prepared and delivered to you, cuddling with someone who loves you, going for walks, and getting scratched and rubbed daily? Sounds pretty fantastic to me!

Again, the caveat being—*in a loving home*. How heartbreaking that too many of these unconditionally loving creatures still find themselves abandoned and abused in the modern era. One of my wishes is that during this lifetime, we see pounds and euthanasia of healthy dogs become an outdated and barbaric practice, never to be revisited again.

The three fur babies in this book, in one way or another, were all rescued. We adopted Butters just before most of his siblings were dropped off at a pound. Lucy was rescued after recovering from injuries believed to be sustained from being thrown out of a moving car as a young puppy. Coco was found wandering the streets by our friend at just four weeks old on a 113 degree Arizona summer day. Sadly, these are probably the least horrific stories out there. If you need any more incentive, please adopt.

Before we get into the insights shared by my faceless friend who spoke to me for three days and hasn't returned since, let me introduce you to the three furry actors that demonstrated countless behaviors to help me gain deeper insight into how we as humans interact, and the possible ramifications of our choices. These invaluable perspectives helped me to view common behaviors in a different light. My hope is that you will find them just as intriguing, ultimately providing you with an outlook that will make life a bit easier, happier, and much more fun.

Without further ado, I introduce you to three of my favorite dogs…

First up, we have my boy, Butters.

Butters

AKA
Lick-a-Lick
Butter Balls
Swirly Butt
BUTTERRRRZZ– when in trouble.

PARENTS: Amy & Rick

BIRTHDATE: November 23, 2013

BREED: Chin Pin (Miniature Pincher & Chihuahua mix)

TRAITS: Stunning eyes, super-fast runner, and only has eyes for his first love—Lucy.

More about Butters from his perspective…

MY PERFECT DAY…sleeping in on a fuzzy body pillow, under a down comforter, until well past 9:00 AM. Going for an hour walk, which includes running off-leash and chasing my favorite blue face ball. Afterward, nibbling on some fruit with mommy in our back yard. Shortly after, eating a meal of the most expensive and 'healthy' dog food made. Sunbathing for a while, chasing and catching a bird, and then napping with Mommy or Daddy again.

I'M A GOOD DOG BECAUSE…I only poop in one designated area on the side yard. My mom gives me treats every time she picks it up. She tells me I'm a good dog because I never bark back at dogs on walks. Mommy and Daddy love when I come and cuddle with them. Whenever they hug, I whine if I'm not included.

I'M A BAD DOG WHEN...I bark at any noise out in front of my house. My mom squirts me with water from a spray bottle and I hate it. But, I can't help myself and I continue to bark at anyone I think is coming near my home. And well, if they knock, I'm even louder. The same goes for the backyard. If birds fly down into my yard, I bark to scare them away. When I do, Mommy and Daddy yell at me to come in and get in my cage. (Which is six feet long and open on the top, and I lie in a bed with a blanket, but I still don't like it because they are unhappy with me.)

I SCARED MY MOMMY THE MOST WHEN...I caught her a bird and brought it into the house through my dog door. She screamed super-duper loud and was not happy with me at all. I thought I was bringing her a present and showing her how fast I was. She didn't seem to care about anything except getting it out of the house as fast as she could. A close second was when I was a puppy and chewed on rocks and doggie poop bags and had to go to the vet numerous times.

Lucy

AKA
Lucy Gucy
Lucy Lu

PARENT: Geani

BIRTHDATE: January 21, 2014

BREED: Terrier & Chihuahua mix

TRAITS: Extremely friendly, wagging tail, perfect posing model, everybody loves Lucy!

More about Lucy from her perspective...

MY PERFECT DAY...sleeping in under a blanket in bed with my mom. Warming up for my day by running up and down the hallway chasing a ball while Mom drinks her coffee. Afterward, I eat my breakfast and take a nap on Mom's lap while she drinks her second cup of coffee. Then we go for a walk, making the rounds to say hello to our friends. In the afternoon, fighting with my sister Alice for the best spot on the couch in the sun so I can take a long nap. The day is topped off when I get my favorite afternoon treat—chicken jerky. Sometimes Mom gives me the ones from the doctor that are good for my teeth instead. They are not quite as good but I don't discriminate and accept all treats!

I'M A GOOD DOG BECAUSE...I stopped piddling in the house when I get excited like I did when I was younger. Mom tried to make me wear diapers when we went to our friends' houses and I was so embarrassed, I stopped. It wasn't worth being dressed up like a little baby. I also come when I'm called, really fast when I smell there is a treat involved!

I'M A BAD DOG WHEN...I get so excited to say hello to my human friends—to tell them how happy I am to see them—that I jump on their legs. Mom is also not happy when I try to eat bones or stray hot dogs on the sidewalk on my walks. I'm really good at sniffing out delicious smelling abandoned meat products. Sadly, I'm never quite quick enough to get any down before she takes it out of my mouth and throws it away. I will keep trying! I also get in trouble when Mom says I keep teasing my sister Alice. She is a cat and licks herself all the time so I thought it was helpful if I licked her face for her where she couldn't reach. Alice swats at me and Mom tells me to stop, but I don't know why.

I SCARED MY MOMMY THE MOST WHEN...I slipped out of my harness and took off running. She seemed so scared because I didn't come right back so now I don't go as far. The next time I tried to slip and run, she caught me and told me that I wasn't Houdini. I don't know what that means but I don't try to run away anymore because why would I? I have the best mom and life!

Coco

AKA
Coco Chanel
Wendy Coco
Coco Puff
Sweet Potato
The Queen

PARENT: Cassandra

BIRTHDATE: July 16, 2015

BREED: Chiweenie (Chihuahua and Dachshund mix)

TRAITS: Green-eyed beauty, hungry, unfriendly to most strangers especially big dogs, but loves a select few.

More about Coco from her perspective...

MY PERFECT DAY...sleeping under a down comforter, snuggled up against a preferred human's neck until about 7:00 AM, going for a walk and then running off-leash. Immediately afterward, I'm ravenous and want any human food—fruits or vegetables—that someone will give me. My very favorite is sweet potato. However, I will eat pretty much any food put in front of me. (There are dogs starving out there, ya know?) Then, I love to play tug-of-war and fetch with a toy that is full of squeakers, followed by some sunbathing. Topping it off with a bully or a yak milk bone makes it the most perfect day ever!

I'M A GOOD DOG BECAUSE...I listen and come when I'm called, especially if I know there is food involved. I'm a very quick learner and I know where to go to the bathroom at one of my favorite humans, Amy's house. I give five when asked to, and I will try to do anything anyone else can do even though I have arthritis in my back left leg. Sometimes I walk on three legs but that doesn't stop me. If you are one of the few people I love, I will cuddle with you and give you lots of kisses.

I'M A BAD DOG WHEN... I growl at other dogs on walks because they scare me. Also, I'm told I'm bad sometimes when I'm not ready to go the bathroom when my mom takes me out, so I go in the house shortly after we come back in. Mom gets really mad when I collect all of the dog bones and won't share with my brother, Bo. I stand guard and protect them, growling if he tries to mess up my perfect pile.

I SCARED MY MOMMY THE MOST... quite a few times. I like to eat anything I can find—particularly cigarette butts while on walks. It made me very sick and I had to go to the doggie hospital and get needles in my leg. Also, sometimes when I run or jump too much, my bum leg that hurts gets so bad that I shake and have to go get pain medicine. I can't help that I'm a dare devil and like to try doing or eating anything I can. That's just part of my charm and I've been told quite a few times that I have beautiful eyes.

CHAPTER 3

Hot Diggity Dog

"'Hot diggity dog' is an old adage used to convey extreme excitement."[3] For me, it describes one of my favorite pastimes—watching Butters run like a wild man.

Most days, I catch myself giggling or noticing that my face hurts from smiling so widely as he races toward me, tongue out and jowls pulled back, as if he is smiling

too. The joy he exudes is so palpable, it's impossible not to feel elated along with him. Geani and Lucy helped me to train Butters off leash. This fills me with immense gratitude because without them this simple yet exquisite pleasure would not have been possible. Previously, I was too scared to try on my own, fearing that he would run away.

During their first few hours together, to say Butters, Coco, and Lucy were excited to run at the park, eat birthday cake, and wrestle with their new toys is an understatement. I thought it may be fun to watch them all play together, but I had no idea at the beginning of this three day event that simply observing them interact would teach me so much.

After returning from the park and eating dinner, it wasn't long before all three dogs fell sleepily into their beds, exhausted from the birthday party festivities. When they awoke the next morning, I was excited because it was Thanksgiving but their collective elation seemed to have fizzled some, similar to partially wilted balloons hanging halfway between the ceiling and the floor the day after a party. After the initial excitement wore off, their true colors began to emerge. Isn't that the way it is for all of us? Most humans are better at pretending for longer periods of time, but dogs, not so much.

During breakfast, which was a wrangling session in itself—trying to get each dog to only eat out of their own bowl—the lessons began. Butters has always been nonchalant about eating and if another dog wanted his food, he stepped back and let them take it. Although I like that he isn't aggressive, I'm not sure if it's always a good thing. Maybe it would be a bad thing if I didn't watch them eat to make sure he got his food. Maybe he knows there will always be more and there is no reason to fear there won't be. Or maybe he thinks if those who are taking it are so aggressive, they must need it more than he does. If I wasn't there to supervise, he would probably change his tune once he missed out on a few meals, eventually becoming more territorial. Who knows?

Unfortunately, the voice that suddenly began sharing his invaluable insight with me as if it was just another regular day in the neighborhood, didn't tell me *what* the dogs were thinking specifically. Instead he mostly pointed out, while they demonstrated, that we all have choices and how those choices can play out in our lives as well as those we encounter along our paths.

Which leads me to nugget number three—*you have the power to choose your perspective and how you approach people and situations that present* themselves in your life. Never feel helpless because you are not—you always have a choice.

> ## Nugget #3
>
> You have the power to choose your perspective and how you approach people and situations that present themselves in your life. Never feel helpless because you are not—you always have a choice.
>
>

Butters has a choice whether to be passive about letting others eat his food or not. Coco on the other hand is completely dominant about eating anyone's food she pleases. Again, why? Not sure, maybe it is an inherent personality trait, or maybe she was so hungry when she was abandoned at a few weeks old that she became sure that when food was presented, she had to eat or lose out. Watching her daily for the first seven months of her life while her mom worked, allowed me to be with her a good deal of the time shortly after she was rescued. At just two pounds, she would eat all of her food and then walk over to Butters' bowl, climb in, and finish eating his food. He would just watch her, allowing her to do it. Butters behavior encouraged hers, although as she grew and was given more food, he learned to come when called and to eat more quickly so he was finished by the time she was. Isn't it funny how we are all motivators for one another? Before Coco was around, Butters would let his food sit until he felt good and ready to eat.

At mealtime and for treats, I prefer to give my dog different fruits and vegetables. Guess who tried and liked everything? Of course, the curious baby, Coco. Didn't matter what it was, raw or cooked—carrot, cucumber, apple, or sweet potato—she was down for it. As his norm, Butters is slower and pickier, but eventually tried all and only shunned the cucumber. Lucy's mom prefers her to stick to mainly eating her food and treats provided, but she not only loved a bite of sweet potato, she dove and caught Butters' piece out of mid-air. She's more of a loving lap dog than a runner so I'd never seen her move so fast! This reminded me that we can all choose healthier treats, especially many more varieties of fruits and vegetables. The best part for those who love to eat is that you can consume so much more of them with only a fraction of the calories.

Don't be afraid to try something new—you never know, you may even find a new favorite treat. Although, there are always exceptions and you may find something you never want to try again. On my never again list—chicken feet. Geani gave Butters his first and last one. He loved it, but my better half, Rick, and I both became nauseated by the loud cracking sounds as he gnawed his way through it. The icing on the cake was when he hid the half-eaten slimy lump in our bed. To each their own, but we don't mention 'chicken feet' in our house anymore.

I told Geani when she returned for Lucy how obsessed she was with coming into the kitchen and smelling the food cooking during our three days together. We laughed because Geani doesn't spend any time in the kitchen so evidently Lucy was confused with the long hours and smells radiating throughout the house. She literally came into the kitchen every fifteen minutes the entire time I was cooking, even though I told her "out" every time, which totaled at least eighteen hours over the three days.

Jokingly, I said Lucy was acting like a crack addict in a crack house. Which reminded me, if you have a problem with abstaining from something—which

I'm intimately familiar having previously smoked cigarettes for over twenty years of my life—stay away from it and definitely don't bring anything into your home that you have an issue with. It's a million times easier to say 'no' to something initially than it is to quit after you've formed a habit. (Quitting smoking was hands down the hardest thing I've ever done, besides bearing a baby over nine pounds naturally of course. That is one time I am now a firm believer in saying 'yes' to drugs!)

After breakfast, the power plays and territorial lines continued being drawn. Butters, as usual, was lying in the middle of the couch like Switzerland, uninterested in the drama between the two girls. Coco energetically collected the bones, made a pile, and assumed the guard dog position in front of them. Lucy, spent a good deal of time sitting against the wall, not cowering in fear yet definitely avoiding any confrontation by staying away from the couch, rug, and play area.

On cooking breaks while watching them, Lucy seemed to want to play. When I called her she would come but she would *not* stay in the area without me. Unlike Butters, who ignored Coco or turned his back to her so she couldn't get to his bone, I could tell Lucy wanted to play but she wasn't willing to stand up for herself. Instead of trying to have fun by telling her playmates when she was uncomfortable—she simply removed herself.

Although I'd hoped that this dynamic would change after a day or two, it really didn't. Lucy continued to avoid the area unless I was present for the most part, although eventually she did lie on the couch or rug, albeit, as far away from Coco as possible unless she was next to me. The philosophy that she preferred being alone couldn't be completely accurate because if that was the case she would not stand watching with interest and wagging her tail at the area where Coco and Butters were. She appeared to want to join in when they were playing, but sadly, she allowed fear to paralyze her.

Coco, on the other hand, was fearless, investigating everything with the openness of a toddler who doesn't know enough yet to feel frightened of anything. There wasn't much holding Coco back from trying new things, appearing unbothered by what others were doing as long as she was enjoying herself. She appeared unable to see a boundary or road block unless given one by me. One could say that she approaches life with gusto oblivious to any obstacles. Some months later, we found out that she has arthritis in one of her back legs which was a bit shocking that at such a young age she was afflicted with a disease that typically affects the elderly. Coincidently, her mom had juvenile rheumatoid arthritis as a young girl as well.

Who can say *why* Coco has the personality she does. Maybe this isn't her first turn around incarnating as a dog, therefore, she goes for it. Many times,

I've been mesmerized watching her grab a squeaky animal toy, waiting for me to play tug-of-war, then becoming joyously lost in having fun regardless of what others are doing. What a freeing way to live…diving right in without limitation, oblivious to anything else. We are told as children to be aware of others' feelings and not to exclude anyone, but there is something to be said for unapologetically doing what makes your heart sing. I admire that about her.

    Regardless of our commendable traits, none of us are perfect, as demonstrated by her guarding-the-bone-pile behavior. If left unchecked her dominance could go over the top into bullying, so quite a few times I had to dismantle her pile and supervise until everyone had their bones and she minded her own business. Although Coco had to be redirected with the bone hoarding, she took the discipline in stride. It was pretty easy to get her to do something else. I don't know if that flexibility comes from her personality or because of her young age, but either way I was reminded by my new faceless friend that when you can't do something one way, it is much easier to just change gears and try something else instead of fighting it.

    On the other hand, Lucy and Butters, both around three years old at the time, didn't go with the flow of redirection nearly as easily. My narrating friend continued by reminding me of what a difference this could make for me when approaching roadblocks in my own life.

Which leads us to nugget number four—*if something isn't working, don't keep chasing your own tail, doing the same thing over and over, and expect a different outcome.*

Not only is it typically fruitless, but as the famous quote Rita Mae Brown wrote in her book, *Sudden Death*, "Insanity is doing the same thing over and over again, but expecting different results."[4] Find another route. Don't get hung up on one way and then lie down and feel dejected because you were told no—which seems to become more likely in older age and with certain personalities. Remember, don't be that old dog that you can't teach new tricks!

> ## Nugget #4
>
> *If something isn't working, don't keep chasing your own tail, doing the same thing over and over, and expect a different outcome.*
>
>

Even though we may prefer certain personality traits, it is important to appreciate one another's differences. Many of us, Butters included, tend to be all or nothing in our lives. When Butters is on, he's full of energy—running and playing at high speed, but when he's done, he is down. At night, he sleeps for twelve hours straight, rarely moving. Coco is more of a grazer—she plays, rests, plays, rests, and for me, as much as I love taking a nap with her, she is *not* a good sleeping partner for more than a few hours because she moves constantly. Lucy falls somewhere in the middle of the two, only moving a couple of times, usually sleeping for about eight hours. One is not better than the other unless it gels more with your habits.

Isn't it funny that these three, with their very different personalities, were brought into one another's lives? Maybe even dogs are meant to come here to learn from one another? The endless possibilities of all that we have the opportunity to experience in our lifetime is truly exciting.

CHAPTER 4

Doggone it!

If you are like me, many years ago you probably heard someone exclaim, 'Doggone it!' when they were frustrated. You may still hear it occasionally, but for the most part the younger generations and the more foul-mouthed older generations, like myself, go right for the cuss words, not cute stand-ins like the aforementioned.

By mid-morning, I'd already prepared and seasoned the spaghetti sauce from scratch, browned the sweet Italian sausage, which was now simmering in the sauce, and prepared the six pounds of meatball mix. I needed a break before taking on the task of rolling more than fifty large meatballs, not to mention wanting a reprieve from repeating myself for what felt like the hundredth time saying, "Coco-stop making bone piles," "Lucy-out of the kitchen," and "Butters! Leave Lucy alone, she doesn't want to wrestle!"

The term 'puppy love'—described in the dictionary as "A state of short-lived infatuation or romantic attraction"[5] is an understatement when it comes to Butters' unrelenting adoration for Lucy. The difference—it isn't shallow and it has stood the test of time. From the first day they met, when Lucy was about seven months and him nine months, he was instantly smitten. They would wrestle for hours while Geani and I tried to chat in between constantly separating them because Lucy's white neck would turn pink from Butters nipping at it, not to mention the high-pitched whine became extremely annoying. We assumed Lucy was the culprit, but eventually we realized that it was actually Butters who was so vocal during their play sessions. Butters never wrestled with anyone like he did with Lucy until Coco came along.

The difference was he would take the passive position and lie on his back and let Coco lead the play, which was the opposite of him and Lucy. Since Coco was only a few weeks old and two pounds when they met, I think he was trying not to hurt her. Again, he loved to emit this whiney noise the entire time they played. It's funny at first, but grates on your nerves after a while. Although Butters loves to wrestle with Coco, they have a brother/

sister vibe. With Lucy, he's tried countless times to consummate that love, much to Geani's dismay.

By the time I was ready for a cooking break, the three dogs were all restless and as ready for their walk as me, collectively jumping up and running towards the door when I asked who was ready to go for a walk. I'm so grateful for the need to walk my dog, as it has required me to take care of myself by getting out every day, which probably wouldn't happen if I didn't *have* to.

This brings us to Nugget number five, which you've most definitely heard before but bears repeating—*if you are feeling anxious, stressed, or depressed—go for a walk. Take it from someone who's felt that way quite often, it helps.*

Luckily, my daughter, Cassandra, stopped by to learn how to make meatballs since I don't use a written recipe. For her first twenty years of life, she had not

> **Nugget #5**
>
> *If you are feeling anxious, stressed, or depressed—go for a walk. Take it from someone who's felt that way quite often, it helps.*
>
>

one ounce of interest in learning or trying to cook at all. Sometimes, she would pretend to help me make cookies, but what she really wanted to do was lick the beaters and then disappear until they were out of the oven and needed taste testing. Although I was sure she still didn't want to learn, I'd asked her to come and help me in the morning since she was going to her boyfriend's house for Thanksgiving dinner later in the afternoon instead of joining us at our friend's house.

This irritated me because I knew she wouldn't be with him more than another year or so until they broke up. No judgment that is how it is at that age, as it should be. What she doesn't understand yet is that you can't get the holidays back once they've passed. For some reason, it appeared that it was more important to spend time with a future stranger and their family than me. Probably another reason I feel extra appreciative for my dog's devoted loyalty at this particular time.

Anyhow, with her walking Coco, I only had Butters and Lucy, which was nice. They'd walked together on a splitter before so after the initial tugging and remembering they had to work together, it went smoothly for the most part. None of the three had the same vigor to run in the field a few blocks over as they did at the park the day before, but they all seemed to get rid of their excessive energy.

Cassandra hadn't seen Coco run off-leash, so it touched my heart when her face lit up as she reveled in the simplistic joy that watching your dog fills you with. The funniest part was that since Coco had been with me for over a week, she'd already grown somewhat accustomed to this unencumbered freedom. In that short amount of time, she no longer took off and ran non-stop like she'd demonstrated the first few times she experienced it. As if she'd gotten used to it and her new norm became running almost daily. My invisible friend reminded me that it is so easy to become blind to all of the gifts that surround us every day until we no longer see how lucky we are.

Which offers us nugget number six—*always try to see each day through fresh eyes. What would it be like if you didn't have what you do now?*

Nugget #6

Always try to see each day through fresh eyes. What would it be like if you didn't have what you do now?

This reminded me to be grateful that my daughter came and spent time with me on Thanksgiving, no matter what time of day or what we were doing. Instead of feeling resentful that she chose a fleeting boyfriend over spending the holiday with her mother, it was much more rewarding to enjoy the time we did have together. That was the true gift.

Cooking the meatballs and finishing in the kitchen for the day took me a few more hours after our walk. I'd hoped that what felt like a thousand corrections in the morning may have stuck and the afternoon would be a bit easier. It wasn't. Lucy continued to come into the kitchen constantly like it was her job. The worst part wasn't telling her 'out,' but the chain of reactions it set off.

As soon as it appeared that all three were contently chewing their bones, Lucy would abandon hers to peek in the kitchen to see if something had changed and she was suddenly allowed to taste test the meatballs. This caused Coco to immediately drop hers to scavenge Lucy's bone, and possibly Butters if it was abandoned, so she could rebuild her pile. Of course this awoke her greedy guard-dog mentality and she would growl at any canine that dared look her way, which caused a second correction on my part. Not to mention that Butters wouldn't give up his plight to wrestle with his lady love. This played out so many times I wondered if unbeknownst to me, we were creating our own sequel and someone was secretly filming *Ground Dog Day*.

I'm not sure why they couldn't seem to each find their place and relax with one another. Maybe it was torturous for them to have to smell the wafting scents of sausage and meatballs that filled our small home without being able to indulge. Or possibly they'd grown tired of all being together for 24 hours, but whatever the reasons, if they weren't fighting over the bones, they all wanted the same toy.

Each had been given a ball in their birthday party goodie bag. Although each ball was a different color, they were the same size and contained a squeaker, but for some reason everyone wanted the blue one. I mean, I'm partial to blue as well, but it didn't make any sense considering Rick said he thought he'd heard that dogs are colorblind.

Curious, I googled it and found that dogs are partially, not totally colorblind—but definitely possess a much smaller range of colors than humans. PetMD stated that, "Dogs see shades of blue, yellow, and green. Which may explain why dogs love chasing a bright yellow tennis ball on the green grass under the blue sky.[6] Maybe that's why they all wanted the blue one because they could see it versus the red and orange ones that appeared grey to them. Who knows?

To me, it seemed ridiculous that all three of them lost out on enjoying their own bone and toy, simply because they wanted to fight over the blue ball. Maybe I couldn't fully appreciate the beauty of seeing a blue hue over grey since although I have horrible eye sight, I am not colorblind. Obviously, they didn't understand me when I relayed what my insightful friend whispered in my ear—enjoy what you *do* have, the grass isn't always greener. They didn't understand so I tried to demonstrate it by showing them what it was like to have no bones or toys. I'm sure they didn't really get that either and just thought that I was mean. The good news was that I *did* get the outcome I was looking for—everyone quieted down for a bit.

After finishing the meatballs and before beginning the vegetable dishes for Thanksgiving dinner at our friends—Doc & Cheryl's—in a couple of hours, I sat down on the couch for a few minutes to rest. That wasn't what my furry friends had in mind as all three of them began vying for my attention. Of course seven pound Coco climbed up on my stomach without hesitation, claiming her front and center position. Butters spun in a circle before plopping down and claiming my left hip, his preferred cuddling position. Lucy gladly accepted the right side and rolled on her back to give me easy access to her belly. Each feigned relaxation, but their wagging tails gave away what they really wanted—some neck scratching and belly rubs. Have you ever tried to pet three dogs with two hands? Not the easiest task especially when you quit petting one and they give you sad eyes until you switch back to them.

With my new invisible friend's nudging, I began to ponder how we all seek attention. Most people want it in some form or another, but dogs just seem to take a more straight forward approach with how they ask for theirs. Some of us don't demand attention from whom we are wanting it, which typically results in less received. Others demand it constantly whenever you are in their presence, and for most of us, this gets on our nerves after a while. Conversely, there are those who entertain themselves and allow you to *want* to come to them. It occurred to me that it is much more appealing to be like the last one.

Although there is nothing wrong with asking for *what* you want, *when* you want it and embracing some assertiveness, constantly taking on the needy role will most likely only cause the person you are seeking it from to feel frustrated. Eventually, this results in the person you most want attention from giving you less and less. This reminded me that there is something to be said for being happy and content with yourself and letting affection come to you.

    As with most things in life, shooting for a happy medium seems like the best choice. You know, that dance that many times feels like the illusive point somewhere between knowing what you want and going after it, but not forcing it and letting it come to you. I don't know about you but mine hasn't yet evolved into a cool looking electric slide, where similarly, I think I've got it and am full of rhythm when suddenly, I miss a step or pause too long and trip over myself to get back into the groove.

CHAPTER 5

Dog-Doo

On Friday, our second full day together, I walked all three dogs by myself for the first time. I wouldn't say, shit-hit-the-fan per se', but we definitely uncovered new challenges with the dynamics between the three of them. Although none went as far as causing physical harm to one another during their walks together, they surely were not opposed to pushing each other around for their own comfort, especially when it came to "doing their business." Yes, humans are not the only ones that have varied preferences for when and where they prefer to "go."

After they ate breakfast, our Friday morning began with preparing the cheesecakes because, as my Italian grandmother taught me, to get the richest taste they need to sit for a minimum of 24 hours (preferably 48) in the refrigerator before serving. My nana knew what she was talking about since she baked an award winning cheesecake. No joke. A food critic once wrote in the *Wilmington News Journal* that she made the best cheesecake in the state of Delaware, where she baked for restaurants for a living at one point. Instead of making her huge 10-inch traditional plain creation topped with cherries, I had recently begun breaking the recipe up into three much smaller ones—one plain with cherry topping, an all chocolate one, and one with Oreo cookie crust, plain center and chocolate ganache topping. The variety allowed me to please most palates, although the last one is consistently a fan favorite.

It was definitely a much more relaxing morning for me while baking with the three fur balls behaving better than the previous day. All of them seemed to be growing more accustomed to being together, displaying noticeably less correctable behaviors. I was grateful for the reprieve from repeating my commands to Coco, who seemed to have grown tired of bone scavenging for her pile. Either that or she was over hearing me reprimand her and watching me dismantle it. Understandably, that was quite a bit of work to see it destroyed constantly.

Although Butters still let Lucy know he was available for wrestling, he wasn't as relentless, instead opting for the more laid-back approach to attracting her attention with long adoring gazes and a slow wagging tail. Lucy had even abandoned her wallflower role and although she didn't cuddle up with Coco, she did lie on the couch, seemingly a bit less stressed by her presence. To my delight, Lucy only occasionally wandered into the kitchen, much less interested in the cheesecake preparation compared to the sausage and meatballs.

After the cheesecakes finished baking and were cooling, the four of us embarked on our much more crowded first walk of the day together. Similar to being in a confined space with more people than you are used to, tempers and patience appeared to run thin from the get go. Walking two dogs previously wasn't overly difficult for me, especially with a splitter on one leash, but this was my first experience using that *and* having a third dog, on a second leash in the other hand. Not to mention that my invisible friend seemed to become much more talkative during times when my attention was fully focused on the dogs instead of split between different tasks. Although

I was worried when the dogs pulled suddenly that my phone would go flying out of my hand and meet an untimely demise if it landed face down on the concrete, I diligently typed when he began speaking. This didn't seem like a choice for me, but more like a compulsion. Kind of like someone was whispering winning lottery numbers to me and it would have been simply asinine to *not* take notes.

Almost immediately, it became apparent that one of the most important aspects of juggling multiple dogs, for me and them, was embracing patience. With one dog, especially Butters who rarely stopped to go to the bathroom, typically we spent most of our time walking along at a brisk pace. During our first year or so of walking together at least once a week, Geani had never seen Butters go to the bathroom, number one or two. The first time she saw him pee, he appeared to be ducking behind a bush for his privacy. We joked that he was acting like a person who will never go anywhere except in their home, with the door shut, when no one is around. With three dogs, two of whom liked to stop often, we spent a great deal of time waiting as one went to the bathroom.

During one of our many stops, my wise narrator reminded me of nugget number seven—*we are all on our own paths, learning best in certain ways and in our own time. This doesn't make one way better than another, except whatever works best for us individually.*

If you are like me, you may view a choice as less time consuming or seemingly less painful but just because we prefer our own perspective, doesn't make it superior to our neighbor's choice. This is true for all aspects of life, whether it is how many times we stop to sniff before going to the bathroom, what type of diet makes us feel our healthiest, or what religion if any, resonates with us. Just because we prefer one over another, doesn't make it the "right" one across the board for everyone. Nor do I believe there is only one path that is the "correct way" in God's or a greater power's eyes. Each path is merely a human interpretation, and the only thing that makes it the right one for you is that it is the one that feels the best.

Nugget #7

We are all on our own paths, learning best in certain ways and in our own time. This doesn't make one way better than another, except whatever works best for us individually.

The scariest part of this venture for me was praying that no one landed in another's dog-doo. Seriously, it was rough going the first time. Since Butters and Coco had walked on a splitter together for a good portion of the previous week, I thought it would be no problem when it was three of them. But, for some reason, with this new dynamic, each became quite aggressive with pulling everyone until they had turned, backed up, went further left or right, until finally settling on the perfect spot to defecate. The problem escalated when the other two didn't notice that one of them was incapacitated in a squat position and they continued pulling and moving to find their own magical area.

With Coco being the lightest and with Butters surprising strength for his whopping 11 pounds, Coco began levitating as he pulled harder. Lucy wanted to go another way, while I was in the middle trying to hold everyone back so Coco didn't become a circus act, flying through the air while pooping. If I wasn't petrified of having to potentially clean poop off of multiple dogs, I would have laughed hysterically. Could you imagine trying to relax and release while someone stronger was pulling on you so hard you became airborne. Poor Coco had to fight to maintain her dignity as I repeatedly scolded Butters to wait so she could finish her business. Unfortunately for her, Coco tended to go two to three times on every walk. I'm still baffled how such a tiny girl creates such a large amount of waste.

Maybe she was angry because of her hostile excretion environment or she wanted to take her power back, but Coco made sure she wasn't seen as the underdog for long by becoming more vocal. This made me ponder more deeply why she growls at people as well as other dogs. Not being a dog psychologist, my guess is that she is scared so she does her little grumbling to warn people off. Maybe this behavior stems from being separated from her mom and abandoned before she was a month old. Although I corrected her with a 'no' command, an understanding of her leeriness washed over me. Having been abandoned by my own mother as a young child, I recognized the instinct to feel untrusting and weary of strangers or new situations in general.

Butters, and especially Lucy, were the polar opposite, again creating a confusing dichotomy for well-meaning admirers. When people walking by approached us, Butters wagged his tail and Lucy leapt towards them hoping for some petting as they offered how-cute-are-you-guys compliments. Then there was Coco growling and backing away, losing her plight to escape as Butters pulled harder to move towards them. While reassuring Coco that she was okay, I simultaneously kept close supervision so she didn't become so scared that she lashed out at the strangers. She'd never done it before, except towards a vet who stuck a thermometer in her rectum (who could blame her), but I wasn't letting her warning signals go unattended. All three of them equally loved the treat they received for their patience after passing friends continued on their way.

Could it be a coincidence that Coco was abandoned and displays warnings of aggressive tendencies? I'm not sure since most dogs we've had have been rescued and none were quite as fearful as her. However, my wise friend reminded me how important it is to do our best to be there for our young impressionable children because they need our help feeling safe and loved if we want them to have the best chance to develop a healthy nervous system. What would our world look like if neglect, abandonment, and abuse were non-existent? I wondered how many less would feel the need to lash out at others through bullying or turn to the plethora of ways so many of us choose to self-medicate.

Although it took most of the first walk of the day for Butters, Lucy, and Coco to gain a rhythm for one another, as they each had their own preferred timing and method for finding the perfect spot to do their business, I was amazed at the generous patience they showed me. When I continually stopped walking to type on my phone, not wanting to lose out on any of the rapid thoughts and antidotes my invisible friend was firing off during our walk, all three of them calmly waited for me to finish and begin walking again.

This demonstrated to me nugget number eight—*don't forget to embrace patience for those around you. Offering them a few extra minutes on your journey won't hurt you and it may even motivate them to offer you a treat.*

Nugget #8

Don't forget to embrace patience for those around you. Offering them a few extra minutes on your journey won't hurt you and it may even motivate them to offer you a treat.

CHAPTER 6

Dog Eat Dog

"'Dog eat dog' is often used to refer to a situation when there is fierce competition where those involved are willing to do anything to be successful."[7] On our second walk of our second full day together, my increasingly talkative friend in my right ear pointed out numerous behaviors that my three furry friends were demonstrating. Specifically, how their willingness, or lack thereof, with considering their partners' wishes affected their own experience.

This immediately led me to nugget number nine—*how we choose to behave—towards ourselves as well as those around us—impacts all of our*

> **Nugget #9**
>
> How we choose to behave—towards ourselves as well as those around us—impacts all of our experiences. Remaining present and aware of our actions allows us to more peacefully co-exist.

experiences. Remaining present and aware of our actions allows us to more peacefully co-exist.

Even with this walk progressing a bit more smoothly than the first, devoid of any potential doo-doo catastrophes, all three still had a great deal to learn from one another. Regardless of having already experienced interrelating in the same close proximity earlier in the day, they hadn't yet fully grasped the benefit of working together or at the very least, being less demanding of fulfilling their own needs and allowing one another to have theirs met as well.

While watching them struggling and with my wise friend's help, a lightbulb turned on for me as snippets of scenarios from my own life played on an internal reel, supporting his next statement. Despite the fact that I'd heard it many times before, I finally got it when he told me that the whole point of having relationships is to learn and grow from our interactions with one another. I don't know about you, but there have been countless times in my life with just about every type of relationship—parent-child, romantic, friendship, boss-employee, and so forth—where in an exhausted mindset, I wondered what the point was.

At one time or another, no matter how much I cared for them or how much we had in common, there always seemed to be a problem or obstacle that caused a divide. Numerous times, I found myself wishing that relationships were simpler and less difficult to navigate. This newfound understanding allowed me to view those uncomfortable times with gratitude for what they taught me, not just disappointment that they never seemed to go smoothly or come easily.

For this second go around, I had unconsciously put Butters and Coco on the splitter and left Lucy to walk alone again. After a few minutes, it occurred to me that I should change it up and give each one the opportunity to walk alone, unencumbered by a close neighbor. Within a few minutes of moving Lucy over into the middle to walk with Butters, allowing Coco to walk by herself, it became apparent that the single one always seemed the happiest. This wasn't really too surprising to me, I mean as much as most of us appreciate companionship, who wouldn't rather explore the smells that appeal to them most, not to mention how much more comfortable it is to relieve oneself when you aren't tethered to someone else.

My wise friend reminded me that regardless if we are in a relationship or not, it is always a good choice to remember to spend time alone as well. Not that we have to spend a significant amount of time remaining single in life, although it is a great way to really get to know oneself, but even when we are involved in a relationship, remember to spend quality time dating ourselves. Whether we have done this or simply witnessed other people in relationships who hardly ever chose to go anywhere by themselves, this reminded me to venture out alone. Not only when performing mundane tasks, but for the fun ones too.

Why? Because we are in charge of creating our own happiness and satisfaction in life. If we constantly rely on someone else to be present or to make our time enjoyable, it's easy to transfer our unhappiness onto them if we are feeling unfulfilled. This may seem simple, but for many of us, it is easy to forget that going for a walk, eating a meal out, going to a movie, or whatever we like to do, doesn't always require us to have someone else to do it with.

As this settled into my consciousness, my unseen friend whispered something that caught me off guard—you alone are enough…more than enough—bringing tears to my eyes. This touched my heart and reminded me of something a wise man told me while interviewing him to help write his book. I could almost see his face and hear him saying confidently—*you are going be the first and the only constant companion you have throughout your entire life, so you better learn to like yourself.*

In recent years, you may have heard more people speaking about the importance of loving oneself first and foremost. For me, this goes a bit deeper, asking us to learn to truly enjoy our own company. Case in point—you can love a family member or friend and want the best for them, yet you don't enjoy spending copious amounts of time in their presence. Sadly, many of us unconsciously feel this way towards ourselves, constantly wishing we were with someone, or focusing on our flaws instead of giving ourselves permission to have fun and develop a passion for enjoying our own company.

Maybe the same line of thought applies to the adage—*learn to love yourself before you can love another.* Maybe, once we master thoroughly enjoying spending time with ourselves, we will be more fun for others to be around as well. With an important caveat of course—that those we are in relationship with have or develop mutual interests. This is an especially important part of maintaining fulfilling long-term partnerships. If you have been in a relationship that has spanned more than a decade, you are fully aware that humans change considerably as a result of learning and growing throughout the years. What initially brought you together may not exist anymore. Some decide to part ways once they no longer have the same wants and needs. That's okay. Yes, really. My perspective used to cause me to see myself as a failure when my seven-year marriage to my daughter's father ended. Gladly, now I see it as more of a necessary change for our mutual happiness.

If you decide to stay with a partner and forge new interests, you will find it necessary to learn the art of compromising. You may not love one of your significant other's hobbies, but you can make an effort to express an interest in it from time-to-time so you can share in something they find deeply fulfilling. For example, my other half, Ricky, has fostered a love affair with comics since he was a young boy. I've never read them, nor do I have any interest, but not only have I learned to appreciate comic-themed movies, I look forward to seeing many of them. (If you have a warped sense of humor, you will truly marvel at Ryan Reynolds masterful and hilarious portrayal of *Deadpool*.)

Your partner's hobby may not impart the same amount of joy for you, but spending time cultivating something that makes your loved one happy can feel just as rewarding. Likewise, they can support you with what makes you light up, thus ultimately creating areas where you love doing some activities together, and some apart, allowing you both the freedom to grow individually *and* as a couple.

The great part about having each dog experience walking on a splitter with a partner was watching them learn that for it to work, they had to become cognizant of the other one's wants and needs. Although it was not their first inclination, eventually they realized that it was much more comfortable to fall into step with their partner than to constantly buck them. Unfortunately, this realization was not embraced by any of them very easily, nor was it consistent.

My faceless friend pointed out that this is not unlike the human experience. For a good portion of my life, I viewed events as right or wrong, good or bad, black or white—devoid of most shades of grey. Maybe this was partially a result of my interpretation of a religious upbringing that demonstrated there was a right way or a wrong way to behave. Consequently, I thought that the only lessons that came from the chosen "wrong" behaviors were pain and suffering, ultimately from the wrath of an angry God for being disobeyed. Gratefully, my old view has since been replaced with the belief that a loving energy, comprised of everyone and everything, is non-judgmental and unconditionally loving regardless of our shortcomings.

Watching these adorable dogs struggle with less than charming behaviors, resulting from each trying to fulfill their own desires versus appeasing those around them, made me realize that none of us are impervious to struggle. Along with my stringent right-or-wrong glasses, I formerly viewed people as happy or sad, without much in between, let alone an understanding of the validity of experiencing contradicting feelings simultaneously. Maybe because for most of my life I've been chronically depressed, there wasn't much in-between, so of course I believed that you were typically either happy or sad. The truth tends to usually fall somewhere in the middle. Whether it is hourly, daily, or weekly, we all experience an array of emotions and the key is allowing ourselves to feel them without getting stuck in any one of them. The only constant is that emotions, circumstances, feelings, and experiences will always change.

Watching these three display unbridled joy, contentment, and peace, as well as agitation, compromise, and even unbending obstinacy, along with the wisdom whispered to me, offered me the objectivity that we are here to experience these range of emotions, learn what works best for us, and choose according to our updated perspective the next time.

Which offers us nugget number ten—
Life is like a symphony, chock-full of a range of emotions and experiences, and it is all beautiful, even if it may not always seem so at the time.

> ## Nugget #10
>
> *Life is like a symphony, chock-full of a range of emotions and experiences, and it is all beautiful, even if it may not always seem so at the time.*
>
>

CHAPTER 7

Dog Days

"'Dog days of summer' is a term that describes the hot sultry weather between July and September when oppressive heat saps most of our motivation to get anything accomplished."[8] For me, it also denotes the times when no matter how much we try to remain positive or give our all, nothing seems to go smoothly. During *my* most difficult struggles, it can feel as rough going as trudging through thick, gunky mud all the way up to my chin.

Maybe to a little less of an extent, this is how I would describe Lucy and Coco's relationship. Although they had mutual interests on walks—smelling other dogs' pee, loving treats, and enjoying the freedom to run, to name a few—this wasn't enough for them to forge a strong bond while walking together on a splitter. Even after being released from their forced partnership and were on separate leashes, the struggle ensued.

As it turned out, no one wanted to walk in the middle of the pack, although Butters appeared to care the least about what position he was asked to take. The girls' struggle annoyed me at the time, but after further reflection I surmised, who could blame them? I was never a fan of being the person in the middle while walking or sleeping in a group of three. Did you ever get that unyielding claustrophobic feeling when you were a kid at a slumber party when three or more of you slept in one bed? Even when my daughter was very young and would climb into bed with her father and me, I found myself unable to sleep in the middle. So the dogs' behavior didn't surprise me, but after more than a few minutes of constantly trying to untangle Lucy and Coco's leashes as each kept to their mission of ending up on the far right, my understanding didn't help my waning patience.

Even after letting them spread out across the entire sidewalk in front of me, both girls still wanted to walk on the right. During their struggles, poor Butters was pulled back and forth between the two of them like a kite on a windy day. While watching them, my unseen friend reminded me that although many of us want to walk on the right, sometimes it would be wise to remember that when you are consistently bullheaded and inflexible, walking a path in life next to you can be a lot less enjoyable.

Every day is different, and some days will go less smoothly than you may like, but trying to remain cognizant of those walking beside you and offering some flexibility can help immensely with navigating your relationships. This doesn't mean always bending to others' wants and needs, but there is infinite wisdom in the kindergarten teachings of the benefit to all when you learn to share by taking turns with those you are playing with. Demanding that you *always* get your preference will undoubtedly lead to fights or eventually, no one to play with.

Continuing to test my no-one-likes-to-be-in-the-middle theory, I kept switching Butters so he was in the middle and the girls were on the outsides. No matter how many times I tried, eventually, it came back to the same thing—each wanted go where they wanted to go, and for the girls—the right-hand side was still their preference. Watching each of them remain steadfast to returning to their preferred position and becoming less enamored with them by the minute, the perceptive voice in my right ear reminded me to never judge someone for what they are doing or what path they've chosen. Without their experience or perspective, how do we know what

> ## Nugget #11
>
> *Instead of judging others, it would be far more astute to take notes and remember if a similar situation ever arises in your own life, use what you've learned to make the best decision for you.*
>
>

we would choose? If we haven't faced some of the circumstances and challenges that others have lived through, we cannot unequivocally say that we wouldn't act the same way.

This leads us to nugget number eleven—*Instead of judging others, it would be far more astute to take notes and remember if a similar situation ever arises in your own life, use what you've learned to make the best decision for you.*

I'm sure there has been a time when you were around someone that you considered a good person, yet you found yourself thinking that maybe you would give up something you love just so you can get away from them. If not, I'm open to your counsel because it would amaze me to find someone who has truly enjoyed the company of every person they've met. Needless to say, my inability to appreciate some people that I believed I *should* like—whether this was because we were related or someone we love is fond of them—has caused me to feel guilt and shame on more than one occasion.

Gratefully, the continued disinterest Lucy and Coco treated one another with, regardless of how much time they spent together, led me to realize that just because we don't enjoy someone's company doesn't mean we are somehow a bad person. For some reason, this never fully sank in until watching two sweet dogs, whom I love dearly, demonstrate this for me. Some people or even dogs are not your cup of tea, and that's okay. Maybe certain dogs, but not all dogs, I mean that would just be crazy.

Maybe because they were so wrapped up in the positioning struggle or they hadn't mastered the look-both-ways-before-crossing-the-street lesson, but (without naming names) two of the three tried to step into the road in front of an oncoming truck. My faceless friend reminded me that we may find our paths less bumpy if we stop focusing so much on the people or petty circumstances that bug us and become more aware of our environment and what magical synchronicities are happening for our benefit. For the dogs, the leash and my awareness helped them remain safe. For us, we are the benefactors of grace in so many situations that we are unaware of.

After the dogs were pulled back and told to wait, they seemed to pay more attention to me and my directives again, allowing the distraction of their competitions to fall to the wayside. As my newfound mentor explained, by placing our awareness on the present moment, we are offered a clearer perspective and with it, an opportunity to perceive the best path for ourselves.

With three sweet pairs of little eyes peering up at me, waiting for me to guide them, my ethereal friend reminded me that when someone is offering their time and energy to teach, lead, or walk you through something, be grateful and try your best not to be a pain in the butt. After a while, they may grow tired of you fighting them the whole way and cut their time with you short.

Without a personal experience or demonstration, it may be more difficult to remember that no one owes you their precious time and energy, with the exception of pet parents, teachers, and parents of young children. They all made a choice to commit to nurturing you, and offering you their best. Many times, their best may fall short of what you deserve, but holding onto that indefinitely will only continue to short-change you throughout the rest of your life.

This leads us to nugget number twelve—*As we become adults, it is important to understand that no one else in the world owes you anything, so when someone offers you their knowledge or experience, it is a gift to be treasured.*

The rest of the walk felt a bit easier, leading me to ponder if this was because of the dogs' willingness to bend a bit more to one another after their initial resistance or because I was becoming more comfortable. Probably a bit of both, but I recalled something I learned from the wise Caesar Millan, The Dog Whisper—*dogs take cues from our energy. So, if the human is calmer and more at ease, the dog follows suit.*

> **Nugget #12**
>
> As we become adults, it is important to understand that no one else in the world owes you anything, so when someone offers you their knowledge or experience, it is a gift to be treasured.

The thought of walking three dogs without incident and remaining aware enough to be a good caretaker, while taking constant breaks to type the revelations prompted by my consort spouting continual truths into my right ear, would have previously seemed impossible to me. This was a reminder to always remain open to trying new things, you just might surprise yourself.

Someone once told me—when I asked her how she became so comfortable with public speaking—*that stretching yourself may feel stressful the first*

time or two, but the more you do it, the easier it gets. Considering my disdain for even contemplating the thought of public speaking, I don't know if that is in fact true in those situations, nor am I currently motivated to want to practice enough to find out. However, this unexpected three-day extravaganza taught me that no matter how much we learn, there is always more just waiting to be discovered. The icing on the cake is that by shifting our perspective and awareness, learning lessons doesn't always have to feel as daunting as the dog days of summer.

CHAPTER 8

Underdog

" 'Underdog' is a name given to a perceived weaker party in a situation, who is in a position of inferiority."[9] Many times we assume that the physically smallest of the group would automatically be the underdog, human or canine. Coco definitely shattered this myth for me. Despite being the tiniest of the three, she was not managed by the other two in the least. Quite the opposite, she ruled the roost and was most certainly the 'top dog,' which is defined in animal behavior terms as "the alpha male or alpha female in a dominance hierarchy."[10]

As the days unfolded and these three dogs continued to impeccably act out scenarios while my unexpected narrator randomly shared his words of wisdom, it became much clearer that there isn't a perfect set of rules or behaviors to follow to find one's personal happiness. Quite rapidly, this was becoming my newfound opinion—that no matter how much of a "good" choice we make, the possibility existed that it can always be taken too far. Coco demonstrated this aspect of her assertive go-getter personality with her bone-pile-collecting behavior. From one perspective, she certainly lives life to the fullest tackling it on her terms and probably with little regret.

However, left unchecked, her compulsion to dominate could lead to her having a very sad and lonely life if she becomes so embroiled in protecting her pile that she doesn't have any time to enjoy chewing her own bone. Not to mention that it isn't much fun standing all alone protecting a pile of bones when there is no one to play with because you've scared them all away.

This offers us nugget number thirteen—*honest self-reflection is a wonderful tool we can use to temper our behaviors towards ourselves and others, before they become detrimental to our happiness.*

My faceless friend chimed in to remind me that although it is in fact a magnificent idea to spend time reviewing our motivations, behaviors, and relationships with the intent to learn and improve, it's also just as, if not more, important to take time to bask in the beauty of simply being. After the last couple of days, it was no longer surprising to me to watch as the dogs simultaneously demonstrated a physical example of his wise counsel. Each had found their preferred space in the back yard to stretch out and soak up some of the warm afternoon sun. The weather was beautiful—cool air with little to no humidity mixed with warm sun—creating what felt like a perfect 72 degree day.

> ### Nugget #13
>
> Honest self-reflection is a wonderful tool we can use to temper our behaviors towards ourselves and others, before they become detrimental to our happiness.
>
>

Have you ever noticed that even in a space with less sunlight dogs will search for the sunniest place to rest? Our beloved late dog, Angel, would find the one ray of sun that peeked through the window into the middle of the kitchen floor in our previous interior townhome. Regardless of what was going on in the kitchen and unless told to leave, she laid in the inconvenient spot until getting her fill. Why? My feeling was always that it was healing, again as long as it wasn't overdone. There is something so satisfying and deeply relaxing about lounging in the warmth for a short time.

    I don't know about you, but simply watching a dog lying in the sun is one of those mundane yet surreal moments that instantly transforms me to a place of peace. Dogs are masters at surrendering and soaking up healing rays. So much so that just the act of observing them is enough to change my never ending loop of thoughts to almost instantly feeling as though I'm floating on a cloud. If you are a person that finds it difficult to quiet your mind, may I suggest that you look for a dog sunbathing and simply watch them. They can help you reach that many times elusive yet tranquil spot where those who meditate love to be.

    Surrendering to simply being isn't something that many of us were taught as children. Instead, to my dismay, our society appears to thrive on believing the hierarchical perspective that to "make it" or become the ultimate success, one must become the top dog or the best in their chosen field. Raised in the United States, this was also my belief until well into my 40's. After some minuscule accomplishments and many more failures by societal standards, it became clear to me that my measurement of success had morphed considerably. Being fortunate enough to watch these three beautiful creatures demonstrate zen sunning for me, as well as having the time to physically join them was a gift that didn't elude me.

This leads us to nugget number fourteen—*slow down and offer yourself the space to enjoy the simple things in life. They truly are the greatest gifts.*

> **Nugget #14**
>
> *Slow down and offer yourself the space to enjoy the simple things in life. They truly are the greatest gifts.*
>
>

How many times have you become completely embroiled in frustration when you weren't getting somewhere fast enough? I am especially guilty of this while driving or when I have a busy day with a mile long to-do list. Wanting to arrive on time or check off all of our tasks can cloud our journey, masking the beauty of simplicity that frames every moment of our lives.

Gratefully, with my three furry friends and my invisible friend's help, I was able to experience these three days as a collection of moments that were so profound it almost felt as if everything was happening in slow motion. You know what I mean—when for some reason you have to let go and allow yourself to be taken along with the current of life instead of continuing to

believe the illusion that you alone are the captain of the ship. Whether these moments are thrust upon you because of shock or overwhelm, or if you are awake enough to tune into them instead of them being forced on you—you will finally experience the continuous underlying current of magic that we call life.

Although my three days with these three dogs were packed—full of cooking, cleaning, and dog care—many times I had to slow down to give my full attention to each task in the moment. While sunbathing next to these beauties, it occurred to me that my mind and intellect were not what taught me these marvelous lessons. Spirit did, through these adorable fury vessels we call dogs. One could say that Spirit is the ultimate underdog, being invisible and all, but when you become aware that you've experienced Spirit's grace, you will have no doubt who is in-fact *the* top dog.

CHAPTER 9

Dog and Pony Show

"'Dog and pony show' describes an over-the-top performance designed to gain approval of a crowd. Wikipedia expands further stating—the name derives from the common use of performing dogs and ponies as the main attractions of small traveling circuses that toured through small towns and rural areas of the United States in the early 20th century."[11]

I find it whimsical that when most dogs want a treat, they offer excessive focus and obedience for a few seconds until they get what they want, before just as rapidly returning to their authentic and less submissive behavior. As I am sure is the case with many dogs, Butters decided after a while that it was necessary to speed things up and get right to the good part—eating the treat.

To accomplish this, he combined all of the commands he was typically asked to perform before receiving a treat into one short burst. This turned into him sitting, lying down, sitting back up, and offering his paw for a high-five in one fell swoop. All in less than two seconds. Maybe he thought if he covered all the bases, he could get it over with as quickly as possible. All that is required now is getting out the treat bag and he offers his speedy combined trio without much more than me asking if he wants a treat.

Since this felt like cheating to me because he wasn't waiting for the specified command, much to his dismay, I would ask him to do just one of them again. He would repeat his trio for me while shaking and whining as if it was truly torturous to wait. As time has passed, he has worn me down some and most of the time now, I simply give him a treat without asking for him to pose. Quite often, he gets a treat before breakfast because for me, that is the most unexpected time, yet what a great way to start the day. After thinking about it, I would find it highly annoying if I had to pirouette every time I wanted a piece of dark chocolate, which is almost daily and sometimes, multiple times a day. Especially because I would most definitely do it incorrectly, forcing me to jump and take it from them anyway.

During one of the treat round ups when I asked all three dogs to sit, my faceless friend nudged me, reminding me that many times we simply perform the way we think someone else wants us to so we can get whatever "treat" we want from them. You can see this behavior in all types of relationships, professional atmospheres, and in most environments where you are interacting with others. Although following guidelines within certain surroundings can help by offering a universal understanding of what is expected for safety reasons, it is important to remember to be true to yourself regardless of what is promised.

Although it may seem delicious for a moment, many times we realize immediately afterward that we set aside our own convictions to receive a fleeting treat. Disregarding your internal compass is a type of self-sabotage and after repeating it enough times, can begin to eat away at feeling capable of trusting who you are and what you intrinsically know.

Allowing someone else's behavior to affect us can also become so all-encompassing that our personalities can change drastically in their presence. Lucy demonstrated this for me, becoming even more apparent after Coco left Friday evening. Saturday morning, we awoke and there were only two. Although initially a vague sense of relief washed over me, especially anticipating walks, it wasn't the same. As ornery as Coco could

> **Nugget #15**
>
> It would behoove us to remember to embrace our inner child more often.
>
>

be with her bossiness, I love her dearly and missed her already. Without her spunky, ready-to-go, playful attitude, the day felt a little bleaker to me.

Once again the wise voice in my right ear chimed in offering us nugget number fifteen reminding me that like Coco, the baby—*it would behoove us to remember to embrace our inner child more often.*

When we are grown, most of the time we forget to honor our always present childlike attributes which offer us the ability to experience pure joy. Until that moment it had been unclear just how much I appreciated Coco for demonstrating this for me because it was something that was sorely lacking in my life. Many times, someone's profound influence on you isn't fully apparent until they are gone. Following up, my enlightened friend added that we never know the impact our actions or even simply offering our presence has on others.

Although I was missing Coco, it became clear that Lucy did not share my sadness. Quite the opposite, she was much more like her old self—freer and definitely more animated. Without wasting her time worrying about Coco, she even began displaying her own dog and pony show traits. I'm not sure if she had been doing them all along and I'd been too busy to notice or if her new found freedom fed her own ornery side, but it became apparent during potty breaks that she was trying to sharpen her sly dog skills. She definitely needed more practice or maybe a whole new approach, although it was quite entertaining to watch.

My term for her guise to trick me was named the pop-and-squat pee. While roaming back and forth to find the perfect place to urinate, she was extremely convincing—keeping her nose down while sniffing out the perfect spot. After a few minutes, she appeared to have discovered the right area and she did the pop—a kind of exaggerated movement akin to us pulling our pants down. Afterwards, she squatted down to the side and appeared to be relieving herself, but her timing was a bit off—seemingly just a smidge too short to have been an actual proper pee. What ultimately gave her away was the way she glanced over her shoulder at me as if to say, *'see I am going.'* I could have sworn after witnessing this for the tenth time that just like a little kid, there was either guilt for deceiving or fear of being found out radiating from her eyes. Thinking that maybe my mind was playing tricks on me, I kept checking to see if the rocks where she supposedly went were wet. They weren't. They were as dry as the rest of the hard desert ground in Arizona.

Eventually, after becoming completely aware of her scam, her pop-and-squat pee antic became quite hysterical. Lucy is loving and sweet, yet not so good at the slick part, but I gave her kudos for trying...over and over again. If you are thinking—poor girl, she didn't need to go—that was my initial thought as well, but turned out that she did, which was made clear as she went in our small patch of grass merely minutes after I'd given up watching her fake pop-and-squats.

I wondered if maybe she thought she could outsmart the system and receive a training treat each time she offered her faux release. Typically, I offered each dog one but only when they went in the side yard where I'd trained Coco and Butters. Having set up the reward system so they received one treat per trip *only* if they went in the designated area, to her dismay, her plan didn't work out so well.

My Saturday was as busy as the previous days, beginning with preparing the rich multi-cheese mixture used to stuff two pans of cooked pasta shells before covering them in a layer of the previously prepared tomato sauce. After par-baking and allowing them to cool before refrigerating them until it was time to cook that evening, I began the less glamourous task of cleaning. Lucy followed me wherever I went, and although she was more chipper than the previous days, she wasn't as interested in interacting with Butters as she was seeking my attention.

It's not so easy to clean a bathroom with a small dog underfoot, so when redirecting her back to the living room didn't work, I had to shut the door to keep her out and safe from the cleaners. Her disdain for being shut out was audible through her sniffs and snorts under the crack of the door. Eventually, long after I would have, she gave up and returned to the living room. My well-informed friend used this scenario to remind me that it is a waste of time to stand outside of a closed door. Throughout our lives, we will encounter quite a few closed doors but just because you may not see them in the moment, there are just as many open ones waiting for you.

Numerous times while passing by, I watched Butters try to initiate playtime with Lucy, but she wasn't having it. For the entire previous week,

What I Learned from 3 Dogs in 3 Days

Butters and Coco wrestled, played tug of war, and chased one another through the house and backyard for a good portion of the day so he was all about interacting. A couple of times Lucy joined him for a few seconds but was seemingly over it just as quickly, plopping down and ignoring him again. Butters tried over and over again, but she didn't give in too often or for too long. Maybe he was confused because as young puppies they played for hours, but she seemed to have a change of heart or at the very least, less stamina.

Once again my friend reminded me that no matter how much you want someone to interact with you, even if they did in the past, you can't force them to. Continually trying to change someone's mind is a fool's errand, leading you to feel down from the constant rejection. Instead, seek out and surround yourself with like-minded people. When you have nothing in common with those around you on a regular basis, life may become less enjoyable—conjuring feelings of dejection and resentment.

Even if you previously shared interests and were fulfilled in a relationship, we all change. This is why if you want to sustain a relationship, it is paramount that you continually cultivate shared interests with your partner. Initial physical attraction will fade into the background after a few years, but you can always create a deeper bond through sharing common activities and interests. My faceless friend stressed that this is not a judgmental right-or-wrong scenario, but a prompt to find compatibility that offers you more opportunities to feel in synch with one another, which in turn feeds intimacy.

This isn't to say that you *can't* teach an old dog new tricks, which Butters demonstrated on our walk during one of my cleaning breaks. Not that one would consider three to be old, even in dog years, but on the third day, he did something he'd never done—defecated during a walk with other dogs around. This may seem typical, but for Butters, it was not. Previously, he'd never gone number two anywhere except in our backyard, in the designated side yard.

Where it became amusing for me although probably not him, was when he was squatting into position and shimming around into the perfect spot, Lucy decided she would not budge from her spot on the sidewalk. Maybe she was so happy to finally be the top dog on the walk and claiming the right-hand side, the thought of compromising was too much. And of course, Butters felt the need to go on his side, the left. Either way, he pulled exceptionally hard against the splitter as he was trying to poop, with her refusing to give up her place. Their standoff turned into the craziest tug of war I'd ever witnessed. Really, I mean typically excreting isn't part of the game when I was a kid.

My invisible friend offered in the same rhythmic cadence and unemotional tone—let your guy poop the way he wants. There was no humor inflected in the delivery making it even more dry and comical. This reminded me of how I used to think it was almost ridiculous that after seventeen years, Rick still demands full privacy, a locked door, and without interruption or dialogue when he "goes." Afterwards, he doesn't want anyone go in, even after he sprays air freshener. Although I'd already learned to allow him to go his way, this was a good reminder that whether we think it is a simple thing, we all want to be comfortable choosing how we like things done. Who are we to interfere with another's perceived comforts?

Always remain true to who you are. Although offering kindness and some forethought about how your actions or behaviors affect others, never feel compelled to put on a show for another's benefit.

This leads us to nugget number sixteen—*Even though you may not know it yet, you are perfect—exactly where you are, being who you are in this moment.*

> ## Nugget #16
>
> *Even though you may not know it yet, you are perfect—exactly where you are, being who you are in this moment.*
>
>

CHAPTER 10

Be like a dog with two tails

"'Be like a dog with two tails' is a line used to describe someone who is quite happy or excited about something, for example—Jenny has been like a dog with two tails ever since she got a new car."[12] During a moment of reveling in the constant tail wagging and unending joy that the dogs exuded, my invisible friend reminded me that the key to achieving lasting happiness is learning to be like a dog with two tails for no reason at all. If you don't know where to start, begin with feeling gratitude for the simple things. Noticing the miracles that have become mundane—you can walk, poop by yourself, eat good food, lie in the sun, play with friends, and enjoy delicious treats—is best.

Are you wondering why if these don't seem like reason enough to feel especially happy? Because, if you base your happiness on—a circumstance, tangible item, a status or title, reaching a milestone, a romantic partner, or the opinion anyone has about you—your happiness can be taken away in a moment along with the loss of it.

Which leads us to nugget number seventeen—*lasting happiness is a gift that no one can give you. It's an inside job that you alone must discover.*

> ## Nugget #17
>
> Lasting happiness is a gift that no one can give you. It's an inside job that you alone must discover.
>
>

As my busy Saturday of cleaning and prepping for Doc's birthday celebration that evening continued, it occurred to me that the constant barrage of noises didn't seem to interrupt Butters and Lucy's ability to relax. Have you ever watched a dog sit silently, seemingly suspended in a state between being awake and dozing off? To me, they emit an incredibly deep sense of peace. They don't need anything, don't have anywhere to be, and appear to be absolutely content in the moment—whether there are birds chirping or not, pans banging or not, or people talking or not.

Although they have many, I think one of dogs' superpowers is their ability to instantly tap into that well of serenity that flows through the center of each of us, but feels elusive much of the time.

While pausing to take in some of their zen-filled air, my talkative friend chimed in reminding me that we all have the same power in our center, which is filled with this contentment, regardless of what is going on around us. When we feel like we are slipping from our peace, it can help to simply refocus our awareness to our heart. I wondered internally—*but how do we get to that feeling to begin with?*

Hearing my unspoken thought, my invisible friend added—even if you have to force it, fake it, or start listing off what you are grateful for, do it until you *feel* yourself dropping into your heart space. Whether you are currently experiencing the reality you wish for or not at this moment, you can always find something to be grateful for—the warm sun on your skin, the food you just ate, the roof over your head, the smile someone just offered you, the ability to hear the music that just made you feel good, the time to watch dogs, and the list goes on and on. Gratitude will take you into your heart. When you are there, you will feel the peace and joy that you want—that you call happiness.

For most of my life, I believed that happiness was something that happened to you. You were born with happiness served to you on a silver platter or given it wrapped in fancy paper and a bow, or provided it through a circumstance or from someone bringing it to you. After countless years of "working on myself" through a plethora of self-help techniques and therapies, this morphed into the belief that we create our own happiness, beginning with how we approach life. From our actions, what we think about, and the words we choose to speak—which is all true. However, this impromptu crash course from my infinitely wise counsel demonstrated through these beautiful dogs that discovering the wellspring of happiness wasn't about me doing anything more. All that was needed was to consistently go back to aligning with the vibration of love that runs through all life. This is what dogs are masters at—remaining in that flow or at the very least, effortlessly realigning with it at every opportunity.

Another area where dogs are far superior to us is their ability to offer love, kindness, and affection without basing their willingness to give on what they will receive in return. Have you ever been upset and your dog got up from their favorite spot to sit next to you and offer you a kiss, their head on your knee, or a steady gaze of comfort? Whether we respond or not, they patiently and loyally offer their attention and unconditional acceptance.

Growing up, many of us were advised about the importance of remembering the *Golden Rule—do unto others as you would have done unto you.* This is still one of my favorite reminders about how important it is to treat someone with the same kindness we would want shown to us. Where dogs take it even further is that although *we* use what we want as motivation for how we treat others, dogs simply offer their love without any expectation. Maybe this freedom and selflessness is why we are so drawn to offer our own unguarded love to our furry friends.

Maybe the problem lies in that many of us don't treat *ourselves* the way we want others to treat us. Maybe we are not angry that others aren't kind to us, but that we don't know how to be kind, loving, and nurturing to ourselves. This is what leads us to look to other people, places, and things to feel loved. Since this never leads to our fulfillment, we become angry that we can't figure out how to meet this need. Until we turn inward, drop our own self-loathing, and allow ourselves to bask in the unconditional love that already exists in the very fabric of our being, we will remain unfulfilled and unhappy.

My ethereal friend interrupted my thoughts and offered that we can change from constantly seeking happiness to simply relaxing into it, all of this with small, simple steps implemented on a consistent basis. No longer surprising to me, his message was delivered while I was offering Butters and Lucy an afternoon treat. They didn't expect a treat or the kind words offered to them, but they liked them as much as we do, which was evident by their wagging tails. Even if they didn't understand my words, they felt the adoration in my voice. This demonstrated for me the grandness of the small yet powerful opportunities we possess every day to offer consideration and love to ourselves.

My infinitely wise friend offered an example by asking, have you ever noticed when you tell a dog they are a good boy or girl, they wag their tail and enjoy it? We all like to hear we are doing well. Instead of looking for praise from others, give it to yourself. *Who knows what you need to hear more than you?* Offering praise to others, even for seemingly small reasons, is also an easy yet powerful way to change others' lives. Remember…whatever you put out will come back to you.

This reminded me of when Rick and I try a new restaurant and love it, we express it to the waiter, the manager, and even the chef if we can. This was something I learned from watching him vocalize his appreciation throughout the years. Many of us find it to be our first instinct to express what we don't like, yet it's an afterthought to praise someone or something when things are going well or as planned, including ourselves. I've learned that the more you practice sharing what you *do* like more than what you *don't* benefits everyone.

Butters and Lucy were much less active and did a lot more quiet lounging throughout the day. I wasn't sure if it was because they were relaxing more into no longer being the sole dog in their households or if it was the lack of Coco's puppy energy. As with most things in life, it's usually a combination of reasons. Although the long busy days were wearing on me as well, there was a part of me that truly missed the energy that Coco had offered us. Simply by being present, her energy had changed the dynamic by infusing the air with a vibrant, youthful, and playfulness that was plainly missing without her.

When asking Lucy and Butters to do something, their responses were even less energetic and forthcoming than previous days. The wise man interjected by reminding me that like children, younger pups are more eager to ask questions, learn, and try new things. Many times as dogs mature, like us, we tend to become more set in our ways and more definitive about having *what* we want, *when* we want it. He reminded me to strive to stay young at heart and willing to experience new things. Honoring ourselves, our preferences, and choosing to nurture ourselves is extremely important, but it reminded me to avoid getting so caught up in my comfort zone that I forget to approach life through youthful eyes.

Lucy's mom came to pick her up as the sun was setting. Watching her run to Geani with a renewed sense of vigor and excitement, I got it. Although Lucy is always loving and affectionate, she seemed a bit less jovial than her norm. When I'd gone away and Butters had stayed with them, Geani told me he was good but he didn't eat normally and wasn't fully himself. How lucky are we that our furry best friends love us so dearly that they clearly miss us when we are gone.

Be like a dog with two tails

Before the evening festivities began, I sat for a few moments in silence and enjoyed the gratitude I felt for the ability to use my hands to create all of the delightful aromas that filled our home. Watching as Doc closed his eyes and nodded with approval, expressing how much he loved the dinner, filled me up. Which was helped physically by the crisp salad, butter and garlic soaked bread, creamy stuffed shells, flavorful meatballs, sweet sausage, and decadent cheesecake that we all overindulged in. With a full belly and heart, I connected with my Nana's lifelong motivation to cook and bake for her family and many others in the different restaurants she worked for throughout the years. Although many do not appreciate the time and energy it takes to feed others, the effort is well worth it when you see the joy your service imparts.

For a moment, while watching Doc open his birthday gifts after dinner, it occurred to me that I also received an unexpected gift this year—feeling a renewed sense of connection to my Nana, who'd passed away the previous December. While preparing this meal, there were numerous moments when I could feel her presence so strongly I knew she had visited me. No, I didn't see her, nor hear her voice as I did my wise mentor, but her love echoed through my heart and hands as I worked. Once again, there was no doubt in my mind that love never dies. This reinvigorated awareness offered me

peace and solace beyond measure, allowing me to set down a bit of grief and revel that much more in joy for all of the years I was lucky enough to have shared with her.

CHAPTER 11

Downward Dog

Although my first introduction to yoga was over a decade ago and I'd seen dogs do this countless times before when getting up in the morning, I didn't put two-and-two together until recently. The downward dog pose looks almost exactly like the stretch Butters does when rising in the morning. You know when their front legs are stretched out flat in front of them on the floor, and their hind legs and butt are straight up in the air as they stretch their back.

You probably already knew this, but I've never claimed to be the sharpest pencil in the box. What I lack in innate intelligence, I've always tried to make up for with perseverance and grit, which doesn't always lend to copious amounts of patience. Case in point, previously, on days when I wanted to get outside quickly, Butters long exaggerated stretches irritated me. Until I finally recognized that he was giving himself that moment to warm up to make sure he was limber so he could enjoy his walk without injury. This reminded me that many times we are too hard on ourselves, forgetting to allow ourselves the time to stretch or rest when we need it.

Butters and I spent the next day lounging in bed, both of us desperate for some R&R after the marathon of food, fun, and friends. Just as content as me to stay in pajamas all day, he only got up to fetch a drink, a snack, or go to the bathroom when absolutely necessary. I love that about Butters—he is a full on wild when it's time to run and play, but just as passionately, he embraces complete down time.

Sunday's spent watching enlightening shows like Oprah's *Super Soul Sunday* and Gaia TV, reading and listening to radio shows or podcasts of people sharing their experiences of finding their purpose and offering valuable insight, and quiet moments embracing myself and what uplifts me has become a most fulfilling spiritual practice that I look forward to all week.

On Monday morning, we returned to our typical routine, and for me, that came with mixed emotions. Things were much calmer and less crazy which offered some relief, yet to my surprise, I felt somewhat deflated. Happiness still floated around from all of the fun we had, yet a touch of sadness sagged below it. This must be an inkling of what mothers of multiple kids feel like when they've all grown up and left home. One moment, you are running in circles constantly going and doing and the next, your world is much quieter.

When the sun rose high enough to begin to warm the crisp autumn air, we set out on our walk. Again, although much less chaotic, I found myself aware of pangs of emptiness where Lucy and Coco had walked previously. How quickly we become smitten by these furry creatures. After some time, it also occurred to me why the quiet sounded so deafening—my invisible friend's voice had fallen silent just as unceremoniously as he'd begun speaking on Thanksgiving morning.

Having become accustomed to paying attention to his insights while watching the dogs, regardless of the gentle breeze coming off of the duck topped lake, the stillness in the air was palpable. Just like a celebration, the dogs and my invisible friend had come in like a whirlwind with all of their differing personalities and lessons and when the party was over, everyone was gone, leaving me to readjust to a more serene existence.

Although I no longer heard his voice distinctly in my right ear, I could have sworn that threads of his wisdom remained like far away echoes, sharing more insight in a less clear manner. More akin to the subtle brush of insight brought to us as intuition, like waves of barely there leftover scents that linger in the air after days of cooking.

Butters had the same pep in his step as always, seemingly content with how things were and showing no signs of the melancholy my mind was wrestling with. Yet another way dogs are superior to us, completely embracing the present moment instead of allowing thoughts to dampen the joy of being in the now.

Without the need to take down my fleeting friend's thoughts nor keep three dogs moving along, the sounds and sights that previously dominated my awareness crept back to the forefront. Once again, gratitude arose in me when Butters did not react to the numerous dogs that barked at him as we circled the man-made lake in an adjacent neighborhood. Typically in many parts of suburban Arizona, homes are surrounded by cinderblock walls that impede your ability to see into or out of the yards. Although it may seem strange, most lots are less than a quarter of an acre so this offers much more privacy to enjoy your small outdoor space. Although as you pass by closely, you may still see tiny noses and paws in the few small openings for water run off at the bottom of the walls.

The homes that surround the lakes have open fences, allowing the resident canines the ability to see who is walking by. Typically most of them, either out of boredom or claiming their territory or both, come to the fence and bark until you are far enough away for their comfort. This reminded me of our sweet late dog, Angel. Although she never barked inside the house, she flipped out, barking wildly when she saw any dogs on our walks. Although I surmised it was a defense mechanism because she was scared, this wasn't welcoming nor relaxing so many times I'd wished for that behavior to stop. Fast forward five years and now Butters doesn't bark at all on walks no matter how much he is barked at. Even when dogs are snarling and aggressive he keeps a stone face and trots along like he's enjoying a beautiful leisurely day. However, the opposite of Angel, if a bird or animal enters his yard or airspace at home, he barks ferociously.

Watching this play out beside the lake was a great example for humans as well, which didn't elude me. The energy we offer affects ourselves as well as those we encounter. Think about it, when someone is angry and directing that towards you, has it ever helped calm that energy by barking back at them? Quite the opposite, this adds to and feeds their anger. As the exceptionally wise Eckhart Tolle explained in his enlightening masterpiece, *A New Earth*, others' pain bodies want to speak to yours, but if you don't react to them, they don't get fed by you so they move on to look for a more willing participant in their quest to exchange pain.[13]

Although it was annoying, the incessantly barking dogs stirred compassion in me because my guess was that many of them are lonely and full of pent up energy from being fenced in a tiny yard all day devoid of a walk. Cesar Millan shares in his illuminating book, *How to Raise the Perfect Dog* that "exercise, along with discipline, and lastly affection, are a necessity for a happy well-balanced dog's psyche."[14]

When my irritation from the barking dissolved into compassion, it was much easier to deal with. Afterwards, I heard their barks as cries for attention so I began saying hello to each one. To my surprise, 7 out of 10 stopped barking when they were acknowledged. This got me thinking that maybe there would be more peace in the world if we stopped judging fellow humans' barking, acknowledged their frustration, and demonstrated more compassion by being kind even when *they* seem anything but. Maybe if they saw us frustrated but expressing it productively by trying to solve a problem calmly, just like a patient parent, this would deescalate many situations instead of escalating 10 out of 10 by barking back.

Just as quickly, it was demonstrated for me that nothing works 100% of the time. One dog in particular didn't care that Butters ignored him nor that I acknowledged him. He continued barking, appearing angry and aggressive. This didn't seem to matter to Butters either way nor did it change his behavior. We should be more like Butters and try to remain unruffled by others barking around us and continue on our own journey regardless of their behavior.

Just past the unyielding barker, I looked down and smiled. One of the unexpected treasures I've found on our walks during the fall and spring in Arizona is enjoying the beauty of the Jacaranda tree. Not long after they bloom and for many weeks to follow, they drop their vibrant purple flowers to scatter across the ground. From the first time I walked across the covered sidewalk this well-known breathtaking quote filled my mind, *"Forgiveness is the fragrance the violet sheds on the heel that has crushed it."* Although this exquisite sentence is most often credited to the late great Mark Twain, apparently, there are a varying possibility of authors.[15] To the rightful author, thank you for creating a sentence that is as beautiful as it is healing.

There is something so satisfying about stepping on the petals while repeating this line that allows the words to sink deep into my soul. Ever since, when I walk over the fallen petals of these particular flowers, I find myself repeating this phrase and actively feeling myself forgiving someone who has hurt me. One uneventful day after practicing this for a couple of years, I became aware that the one person I'd never forgiven was myself.

Although we often hear about the importance of loving ourselves first so we have it to share, there seem to be many less reminders to forgive ourselves often and fully. Many times below our frustration, anxiety, and unhappiness there are unconscious beliefs that somehow actions that we have taken are unforgivable. Or at the least, self-blame that we should have somehow known better. All that we can do is get up each day with the intention of doing the very best we can. Expecting perfection or to know better without having previous experience is an unending trap. No one has said it as perfectly as the iconic Maya Angelou said to Oprah, "When you know better, you do better."[16]

Which leads us to nugget number eighteen—*Happiness shines brilliantly, yet often lies quietly and unseen just below the dark unyielding layers of regret.*

From what I've experienced, when you clear the dead leaves of misconception away, there isn't much you need to do except sit back and enjoy the perfection that already exists inside you. At the end of the path just past the lake, Butters and I turned in the opposite direction than we typically walked, offering us both new sites and smells on our way back home.

Nugget #18

Happiness shines brilliantly, yet often lies quietly and unseen just below the dark unyielding layers of regret.

CHAPTER 12

For the Love of Dogs

Not too long after our lone three-dog, three-day adventure, Coco and then Lucy, followed by other neighborhood furry friends Spencer & Rizzo, moved away. Used to regular walks and visits with them, Butters seemed a bit lonely. One day as we walked by ourselves, we happened upon a stranger in the field close to our house. She was trying unsuccessfully to convince her dog to play fetch with a little rubber squeaky ball. He wasn't interested but to my initial embarrassment, Butters decided he was. As her dog ran off in another direction in pursuit of swooping birds,

Butters retrieved the tiny blue face ball and claimed him as his instant new best friend.

I tried scolding him to leave it because it wasn't his, and although he typically follows commands by the second or third request as my voice 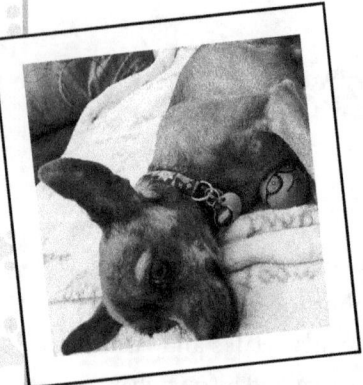 grows sterner, he refused to put it down. Seeing how smitten he was, she generously offered for him to keep the ball. For the next few days, he took it everywhere with him, even to bed.

A week later, he'd chewed through it and destroyed it, retrieving the squeaker as he did with plush squeaker-filled toys. Gratefully, the stranger had told me she was happy to gift him the adorable squishy, funny face ball since it was only $2.99 at Petco. On my next trip there for his nail trim with Traci & Ali, I bought two—one to return to the lady who gifted it and another for Butters. This one was green but he loved it just the same, although in the future he continued to show just a bit more excitement for the blue one. After destroying the first, he never chewed through another one, treating them with the gentleness of a beloved friend.

That day in the field, Butters didn't have any interest in the dog, just his ball. This reminded me that we like who we like, regardless of how big or little, what color, or if we come from different worlds. We love who we love and no one has the right to judge our choices. From the start, it was evident that Butters and his blue face ball were going to be friends for a long time to come. (Sadly, while writing this, Petco stopped selling this ball. Butters refused to chase any other kind afterwards although we tried the same size tennis balls and others containing squeakers to no avail. Luckily, I found them online before they were completely discontinued. Wish me luck finding an alternative after those are gone.)

Needless to say, the face ball became a staple on our daily walks from then on. Many days we walked through the field where we played until he was somewhat worn out. Often I wished I had one of those contraptions that catapulted it further because he runs so fast that he barely breaks into a full run before getting to it, but they come with harder, non-squeaking balls.

At the time, I was in physical therapy for my right shoulder and dominant arm so I had to throw his ball with my left arm, which was quite comical to watch. One time, I meant to throw it one way but it went in a whole other direction. Butters looked confused but quickly set off looking for it. While watching him, I noticed that his tail wagged even more fervently as he searched, seemingly just as happy about having to find it versus just playing fetch when he knew where it landed.

    As time went on, I could have sworn that he didn't look where I was throwing or kicking it so he could do his sweeping circles to search for his precious friend. Once he found it, he ran to me with a bounce in his step, proudly squeaking his way along. After it occurred to me that he enjoyed the searching aspect sometimes more than merely playing fetch, it became my norm to throw it in the opposite direction than he thought.

    One day, as I watched him search, amazed that he didn't see the straight throw, a lightbulb went off for me. Most of my adult life I'd wished to be psychic or know the right answer. At the very least, I wanted to have someone who would tell me what the best option was for me when faced with a choice. To my dismay, even after falling in love with a man who is psychic, he not only wouldn't tell me what to do and how to do it, but he made it clear after a few years that he would not do any readings for me going forward. When I asked why, he told me that he knew the universe took crutches out of our lives if we became too dependent on them. Since he didn't want to be taken out of my life, he would no longer offer me any guidance.

    I thought it was unfair but wanting him as my life partner more than a medium or psychic reader, I agreed. While watching Butters run through the field with his tongue hanging out and tail swishing back and forth, I realized that is the whole point of life. To go out there, have fun, enjoy ourselves, search for what we like, and feel proud when we find it. Just as Butters had grown bored with simply fetching, it would be the same if we knew everything that was going to happen beforehand.

The fear that I'd attached to the unknown was actually the main reason for living and if approached with the right attitude, the joy of life. We are here to learn and grow, and as we all know, unless you've experienced something yourself, you can't truly understand it. No matter how many times someone tells you something, it doesn't fully click until you feel the emotions involved while in the experience.

Wow, this realization was just another day that made me realize that dogs are one of the greatest gifts offered to us. For me, there isn't a wiser teacher. Not because we don't learn from everyone and everything, but many of us are so much more open to the lessons from our dogs because we know they come from a place of pure, unconditional love. No matter what most people say, human relationships usually have conditions.

On another day, after an uncharacteristically deep meditation, Butters and I set out for our walk. As usual, we ended in the field by the church. At first, it seemed like a usual day where he ran, chased the ball, and checked out new smells. Just as we were about to leave, he ran in the opposite direction, stopping under a distant tree. In an exaggerated manner, he seemed to be slowly pushed down by an invisible force until he laid all the way down. In the past four years, we'd lived in the same house and walked daily but he'd never done this. I felt an urge to sit next to him, so I followed suit. After a few moments, I looked down and immediately smiled...we were sitting on a huge patch of clover. In spite of my natural skepticism, I knew this couldn't have merely been a coincidence.

In my mediation prior to our walk, I'd felt my deceased brother, Craig's presence, to whom I'd expressed disappointment in myself for not feeling like I was really accomplishing anything of importance in my life. In a rare instance of clarity and feeling as if he was actually communicating with me, he'd shown me flashes of the things I'd contributed and who they'd helped or touched in some way. Now, here I was sitting on a huge patch of clover.

My left hand reached back and touched the small four-leaf clover tattoo that has adorned my right shoulder since a few years after he'd died. As always, it reminded me of the inspiration to get it. When we were young and took breaks from weeding the garden or to rest on a hot summer day, we laid in the yard. Maybe not every time, but it seemed like it to me, he always found a four-leaf clover in a sea of three-leaf ones. On the other hand, while with him, I'd never found one.

On this day, right after feeling a connection with him, Butters had led me to this very spot, reminding me of those summer days we'd shared. Coincidence? Once again, I was reminded that dogs are smarter than we are. They follow Spirit's lead and bring comfort and joy to us. As happy tears wet my cheeks, I looked into Butters' green eyes, that reminded me of Craig's, and wondered if he understood what he'd done for me. Just in case he didn't get it, I scratched his back and told him I loved him.

Some of my happiest moments, most enlightening experiences, and purest joy have come during time spent with dogs that I love. The ones I've been lucky enough to know have been a shining example of what I've always strived to be—kind, loyal, and unconditionally loving. What they've taught me through my failure to attain their level is that I don't have to "strive" to be like them. Instead, by simply relaxing into being ourselves, we can revel in the fact that we are already all of these things inside. This simply eluded me until seeing it reflected back to me in the eyes of a dog.

What I Learned from 3 Dogs in 3 Days

Maybe a dog's purpose on this Earth is to demonstrate what unconditional love looks like for us so we have an example to emulate. Maybe their eyes are a mirror so we see who we truly are inside our core, where we are devoid of the onslaught of programmed beliefs of self-loathing, and only pure love exists. Maybe if we spend enough time looking into dogs' eyes, we will finally see who we truly are. Then we may become clear enough to wisely choose to treat ourselves and others with the powerful grace of deep and unrelenting love.

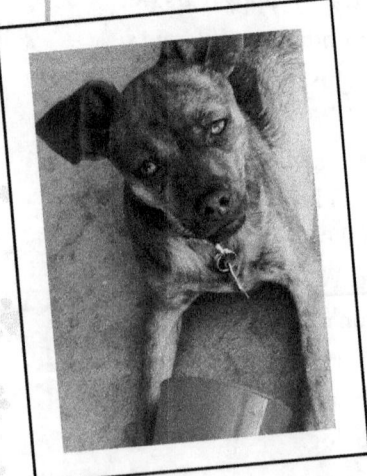

What I learned from three dogs in three days is that if we take more cues from our dogs, we can make ourselves and by extension, others abundantly happier. Now go, find the closest dog to you, look into their eyes, and allow yourself to relax and open up until you feel the immaculate essence that connects us all. After you become rooted in that love, give them a treat or two and play catch with them because whether you know it or not, they've earned it and so much more.

Our last, but definitely not least nugget of wisdom—*Dogs are a daily reminder to keep coming back to the present moment and allow happiness to fill you right now.*

Nugget #19

Dogs are a daily reminder to keep coming back to the present moment and allow happiness to fill you right now.

Epilogue

Why had this wise voice visited *me* for three days? When he began talking, I was so busy that I didn't have time to wonder who *he* was or why he spoke to me. A few months after his voice fell silent and has yet to return, I began to ponder these questions. Through some brief flashbacks, I was eventually able to put them in order and it began to make sense.

Let's rewind about a year and you would have found me at a weekend workshop with Julia Cameron, the author of *The Artist's Way*. Gratefully, a friend, Connie, had invited me to join her to delve deeper into surrendering to the artist within. Having thoroughly enjoyed the book and always open to learning to connect more deeply with my ability to express myself through writing, I readily accepted. The experience was a positive one, helping me to practice letting Spirit guide my artistic endeavors. Although, a brief and public interaction with the author wasn't what I'd longed for.

Having recently finished writing my second book, I was intrigued with a statement she made that all of *her* books were written with the assistance of a voice speaking in her ear. Not only did this fascinate me, but I was jealous and wanted someone to do that for me. This interested me so much that I put aside my extreme disdain for speaking in public, raised my hand, and asked Julia a question.

When she called on me I said, "When I write, information feels like it flows down through my head to my heart and out through my hands. I find this difficult and would really like to have a guy talk in my ear like you." (Many times the feelings that were coming through seemed confusing and difficult to decipher, causing me to question if I was in fact interpreting what I felt accurately.)

Julia's response seemed a bit curt and not what I expected, "You should be grateful for what you get instead of wishing for what someone else gets."

Epilogue

Taken aback and feeling as though I got my hand smacked by a stern grandmother in front of 100 plus people, I was embarrassed. Wanting to forget my humiliation, I didn't think about it again until a few months after the wise voice had visited me on Thanksgiving Day.

Although this partially explained why I'd heard a voice speak in my ear for the first time in my life, my curiosity wasn't fully satisfied. Still wondering why my fleeting faceless friend spoke to *me* and shared all of his wise counsel, another picture flashed through my mind from a few months prior. Struggling with chronic health issues as well as depression and anxiety, regardless of how much time and energy I put into healthful living, motivated me to try a session with an alternative healer named Dr. Karen Kan. I'd come across her inspiring book, *Guide to Healing Chronic Pain - A Holistic Approach*, that detailed how she'd healed from fibromyalgia and chronic fatigue. A method that she used called 'Body Code' intrigued me. After a particularly challenging week, I decided to call and see if she could help me.

During our appointment, while inquiring about some physical issues I was struggling with, she mentioned that the origin was deep-seated anger that was passed down through my paternal blood line for many generations. The reference to anger did not shock me at all, but it did surprise me when she said that I could heal this—not only for myself but for all who came before and after me. I readily agreed.

Since there wasn't really a way to validate anything, after we'd hung up, I began questioning whether this was in fact accomplished. About an hour after my appointment while running some errands, my answer came suddenly when unassisted my car radio volume went from low to high just as the band Switchfoot was singing about not wanting to fight the wars of our fathers. Chills covered my body and for a second I would have sworn over my right shoulder that I saw a line of men's hands on the shoulder of the one in front of them.

While sharing all of this with Rick the following day, I exclaimed how thoroughly exhausting healing work is. I'd been doing this for myself for many years, but I wondered out loud if I was going to do this for all these people, couldn't they send their thank-yous via money. This girl has bills to pay.

A few months later, on Thanksgiving morning, this man's voice sprung up, seemingly out of nowhere. But was it really a coincidence? Or was it a thank you, in the clear man's voice that I'd asked for? Maybe they couldn't shower me with cash or write me a check, so they offered me advice through something I love to do—writing, so I would have a story to share.

Epilogue

This experience demonstrated for me on the deepest level that our own happiness, satisfaction, and purpose is to share with others so they may feel inspired to share their purpose as well.

What will you ask for?

Acknowledgements

Thank you to Spirit for speaking loudly and clearly in my ear so I could hear your words of wisdom. I am so humbled and grateful to be your messenger.

Thank you to Butters, Coco, and Lucy for offering your superb acting services during these three days and for sharing your love and kindness with me.

Thank you to Geani and Cassandra for the time and opportunity to learn from and love your fur babies.

Thank you Sharon Morris for your editing assistance and support, it is so appreciated.

Thank you to Stephanie for being one of my first readers and offering your feedback and encouragement.

Thank you Cassandra Butler for lending your picture editing skills and sharing your beautiful Coco with me.

Thank you to Anne Noser for your wise mindfulness skills counsel that helped me to articulate some of the tools Spirit spoke of so I could more eloquently share these messages. And of course, for your belief in me and this book as it was created.

Thank you to Ricky for always supporting me in so many ways, allowing me to heal, learn, and grow by following my passions. You are my earth angel and I feel so lucky to love and be loved by you.

Last but not least, thank you to my higher self for never giving up on me and continually nudging me to take the next step. You rock!

About the Author

A.P. Morris shares her personal experiences with the hope of helping others.

Her first book, *They're Not Gone*, details fourteen stories, including her own, about how reconnecting with her deceased brother through Psychic Medium Ricky Wood changed her outlook on life & death.

Her second book, *Unwrapping Me*, details her journey to discovering self-love, which was hidden beneath sadness, sickness & self-loathing, through the enlightening "answers" that she received during meditation.

Her third book, *What I learned from 3 Dogs in 3 Days,* offers an account of her three-day dog sitting adventure. To her surprise, as the dogs interacted, an unexpected voice began speaking in her right ear, offering simple yet profound nuggets of wisdom about how to live a happier life.

She lives in the East Valley of Phoenix, Arizona.
You can contact her at amy@apmorris.com
www.apmorris.com

Notes

1. Three dog nights. *Farlex Dictionary of Idioms*. (2015).
   from https://idioms.thefreedictionary.com/three+dog+nights

2. Dog's life. *Dictionary.com*. Houghton Mifflin Harcourt Publishing Company. (1995).
   from https://www.dictionary.com/browse/dog-s-life

3. Hot Diggity Dog! *Dictionary.com*. Houghton Mifflin Harcourt Publishing Company. (2019).
   from https://www.dictionary.com/e/s/dog-idioms/#hot-diggity-dog

4. Brown, Rita Mae. *Sudden Death*. Speakeasy Productions, Inc. Bantam Books. (1983). Pg. 68.
   from https://www.amazon.com/Sudden-Death-Rita-Mae-Brown-ebook/dp/B004QZ9V9Q/

5   Puppy love. *Farlex Dictionary of Idioms.* (2015).
    from https://idioms.thefreedictionary.com/puppy+love

6   What Colors do Dogs See? By Monica Weymouth. *Pet MD.* (2019).
    from https://www.petmd.com/dog/general-health/what-colors-do-dogs-see

7   Dog Eat Dog. *Farlex Dictionary of Idioms.* (2015).
    from https://idioms.thefreedictionary.com/dog+eat+dog

8   Dog days. *Farlex Dictionary of Idioms.* (2015).
    from https://idioms.thefreedictionary.com/dog+days

9   Underdog. *American Heritage® Dictionary of the English Language, Fifth Edition.* (2011).
    from https://www.thefreedictionary.com/underdog

10 Top dog. *Farlex Dictionary of Idioms.* (2015).
    from https://idioms.thefreedictionary.com/top+dog

Notes

11 Dog and pony show. *Wikipedia*. (2019).
    from https://en.wikipedia.org/wiki/
    Dog_and_pony_show#cite_note-circus-2

12 Be like a dog with two tails. *Farlex Dictionary of Idioms*. (2015).
    from https://idioms.thefreedictionary.com/
    be+like+a+dog+with+two+tails

13 Tolle, Eckhart. Chapter 5, "The Pain-Body." *A New Earth*.
    Penguin Books. (2005, 2016). Pg. 144-145.
    from https://www.amazon.com/New-Earth-
    Awakening-Purpose-Selection/dp/0452289963

14 Milan, Cesar with Jo Peltier, Melissa. Chapter 9, "Smells Like Teen Spirit." *How to Raise the Perfect Dog: Through Puppyhood and Beyond*.
    Three Rivers Press. (2009) pg. 260.
    from https://www.amazon.com/How-Raise-Perfect-
    Dog-Puppyhood/dp/0307461300/

15 Forgiveness Is the Fragrance the Violet Sheds on the Heel That Has Crushed It. *Quote Investigator.* (2013). from https://quoteinvestigator.com/2013/09/30/violet-forgive/

16 Winfrey, Oprah. "The Powerful Lesson Maya Angelou Taught Oprah." *OWN*. Oprah's Life Class. (2011). from http://www.oprah.com/oprahs-lifeclass/the-powerful-lesson-maya-angelou-taught-oprah-video

www.ingramcontent.com/pod-product-compliance
Lightning Source LLC
Chambersburg PA
CBHW060515300426
44112CB00017B/2674